MEMOIRS OF AN
OLD BALLOONATIC

Memoirs of an
Old Balloonatic

GODERIC HODGES

WILLIAM KIMBER · LONDON

First published in 1972 by
WILLIAM KIMBER AND CO. LIMITED
Godolphin House, 22a Queen Anne's Gate
London SWIH 9AE

Copyright © 1972 Goderic Hodges
SBN 7183 0302 4

*Typeset by
Specialised Offset Services Ltd., Liverpool
and printed in Great Britain by
W. & J. Mackay & Co. Ltd., Chatham*

Contents

List of Illustrations

*All photographs unless otherwise stated
are the copyright of the Imperial War Museum*

*I would like to thank the photographic staff of the
Imperial War Museum and the Librarian of the Royal
Aeronautical Society, Mr. A.W.L. Nayler, for their
generous help in selecting photographs to illustrate the
book. I also owe a great debt to Miss Amy Howlett of
Messrs. William Kimber without whose midwifely care
this little book would undoubtedly have failed to see
the light of day.*

G.H.

Introduction

Why did I write this book? I did so in the first place about six years ago, thinking of it as a family record. Then one day it occurred to me that it might interest other people, if only a few, that it would be a contribution to the history of that Great War. It would throw a little light on the lives of those who daily watched from balloons.

Brought up in a Christian household, as a young man of 21 I found myself faced with the problem of war and peace. Instinctively I felt that I could not accept the views of pacifists, much as I respected them and still do. Governments are not all of equal value. Being an Englishman, I believe with all my heart that freedom is something that matters. The right to think, the right to speak, our Constitutional Monarchy, our parliament, the knowledge that I cannot be arbitrarily arrested and held indefinitely without trial, all these things are so precious that a man must be ready to suffer and to die for them, if need be. Though I still think of the desolation of war and the death of my friends with horror, I have not changed my mind. I am not ashamed to have served.

The systematic use of balloons for observation was only an episode. Already in the American Civil War a balloon had been so used. But this was a round one. When a round balloon is tethered, it rotates slowly, this makes observation difficult.

A German solved this problem by using a sausage-shaped balloon, and finally a Frenchman provided a reasonably stable platform by using a stream-lined balloon, the Caquot.

In the very beginning of things, before the war, balloons and I believe the early airships were handled by engineers. Long before I arrived on the scene in 1916, all balloon units had become part of the Royal Flying Corps. This, unlike the later RAF, was not a separate arm, but a corps in the Army. It wore khaki, but in a special form, the double breasted tunic, which was striking and, I thought, practical. Officers from other regiments seconded to the RFC were allowed to wear the badges of their regiments, and most did so. I always did so. I had been through Gallipoli with those badges, the Northamptonshire Regiment, the Castle and Key of Gibraltar, Talavera, the laurel wreath. They were a link with splendid men and dear friends. But I loved the RFC too. When the RAF came into existence in April 1918 it swallowed up the whole of the RFC and the RNAS and produced a new uniform for itself. It set to work to produce a new loyalty and a new pride, which might perhaps be said to have culminated in the glory of the Battle of Britain in which the RAF saved Britain and the liberty of all men.

A balloon wing was divided not into squadrons and flights, but into companies and sections. The wing-commander was a colonel. The 2nd Wing with which I served covered the front of the 2nd Army, from the North Sea to the French frontier, though on occasion we could move southwards to help the 1st Army in France. To this day I have a clear mental picture of the area behind and to the south of Kemmel Hill, notably of Messines, and have an odd and special affection for it.

In 1916 wireless was still at a relatively elementary stage. An observer in a plane had at best a small set with which he could send Morse signals. There was no radio-telephony. The balloon-observer had a real telephone-set, linked by cable to his own exchange down below. He could speak to the man at the gun, to balloons north and south of him. His Wing-Commander could talk to him, as could his Company Commander. His exchange was linked with the nearest Army Exchange, so that not only could he speak to batteries and batteries to him, but Corps H.Q. could speak to him direct, if need be.

With direct telephone communication and a relatively stable platform he could direct a shot and observe accurately every shot. When not so engaged, he could keep an eye on the country ahead and note every sign of activity. The fastest planes in those days didn't do more than 100 mph, so that he had time to parachute, for he could see the enemy coming, except on days when the German fighters just dropped out of the clouds. That was just too bad.

It happened to a balloon up in the North; I heard the story from Lee, my neighbour in Flanders, whom I met by chance in London. 'There was a ceiling of cloud. A Hun dropped out of the cloud, shot them up. They parachuted, landed in Dickebusch Lake, and were drowned. I was brought up to take command for the time being, someone else was sent up as second in command.

'A new balloon was brought up and the following afternoon we went up, just to make it plain to the Germans that we were still there. There was a ceiling of cloud. We realised that we were flying at the same height as they had been the day before. The wind was blowing at the same speed and in the same direction. If someone dropped out of the cloud and shot us up, we should land in Dickebusch Lake and we should be drowned. My dear chap, we spent three hours doing that bloody sum, trying to find a mistake, but there wasn't one. We were always drowned.'

Balloonatics, like other soldiers, had to develop their own special type of humour.

1. From Peace to War

A few years ago my younger sister, who in the first World War drove Crossley cars for the RFC and RAF, was talking to young women who, in the second war, had served with the WRAF. One of them said, 'There were no balloons in the first war.' My sister said, 'Oh yes, there were! My brother commanded a balloon unit.' The girl replied, 'He can't have done. There weren't any!'

I am not qualified to write an exhaustive history of ballooning, in peace and war, but I have a good memory for scenes and conversations and can give a simple account of my own happy ballooning days.

How did I ever come to balloons? That's rather a long story. In August 1914 I had been reading theology for two years at King's College, Cambridge, having as my director of studies that great and lovable man, A.E. Brooke, at that time Dean, later Provost. I was a Lance-Corporal in the Signal Company of the Cambridge University OTC.

On August 4th 1914 I was at Rusper, in Sussex, the guest of the mother of one of my two great schoolfriends, Denniston. The other one, Buchanan, was there too. It was the first time we had all been together since we left school. Buchanan, a medical student, was a gold-medallist at Edinburgh University.

He was commissioned in the University Officers Training Corps. The only time he could find for his riding lessons was early on Sunday morning. He was back and changed in time to go to church at eight o'clock. Denniston had been studying abroad in the hope of offering himself as a candidate for the Foreign Service.

A few years before this Lord Roberts had been down to address the boys of Bedford School, then still known as Bedford Grammar School. He urged the necessity of conscription and spoke eloquently of the imminent danger of war. The next day we all three joined the OTC. At Cambridge I joined both the Signal Company and the King's College War Game Club. I was drifting, not realising what a profound spiritual cleavage these contraries could produce in a man; on the one hand theology, on the other the War Game Club.

War having been declared, we all travelled together from Rusper to London. There we parted, Buchanan to go up to report in Edinburgh. I never saw him again. This intensely vital person was killed by a stray bullet in the head at the Helles end of Gallipoli. Denniston went off to join the Inns of Court OTC. After being wounded with the 10th Black Watch, he was killed as bombing officer of the first Black Watch. Before that happened we did have the happiness of a leave together at my home in Derbyshire. How the little children enjoyed having this great big man in his kilt to join in their games at their Christmas party. There was never a kinder man than he.

I went back to Cambridge, was directed to the hall of Corpus and was told to apply for a commission. I was told, 'The Territorial Army is short of signalling officers. You are in the Signal Company. You'd better apply for a Territorial Commission.' After a medical examination I went home, along the charming little line from Cambridge to Kettering, which no longer exists.

A month later came orders. Having equipped myself with the sum provided for that purpose, I was to report to the Adjutant of the 4th Battalion, the Northamptonshire Regiment, at Beyton, a village near Bury St Edmunds.

August 1915 saw me in Gallipoli, first at the Suvla end, then on that most evil Hill 60, to the left of the Anzac position. After five weeks I came off from Anzac with acute paratyphoid. They thought I was going to die that night, but I didn't.

The summer of 1916 saw me back with the regiment in the Sinai peninsula. I now felt a very seasoned warrior, as did everybody who had been in Gallipoli.

I was a firm believer in the principle that young officers should always volunteer for everything. While I had been with the reserve battalion, there had been an opportunity to volunteer for the Indian Army, and one chap had done so. I had been tempted, but after Gallipoli I felt so closely bound to the battalion that I could not leave it when away from it. I must first get back to it. Then, under my own Commanding Officer, I should not feel I had let the regiment down if I volunteered for anything.

An order came round saying that it was proposed to start a flying school in Egypt, and inviting applications. I put my name down. Our Commanding Officer was that great and lovable man, John Brown, later Sir John Brown KCMG, who in the Second War was Director of Welfare for the Army.

He sent for me and said, 'Hodges, have you got a grouse?'

I said, 'Of course not, Sir. I couldn't be happier than I am here. I happen to believe that young officers should always volunteer for everything.'

He said, 'Well, I think you're right. I'll let you go.'

After a long interval orders came to cross over to Suez, spend a night there and catch an early morning train to Ismalia for an interview. In the anteroom of the RFC mess at Ismalia was a mixed bag of subalterns, glaring at one another. In 1968, fifty-two years later, I had the pleasure of meeting one of them, an elderly Yorkshire farmer, when lunching at the house of his son-in-law in the peaceful town of Pocklington, in the middle of which stands a most splendid church. If it had been in Sussex, Fleet Street would have written it up, but it is in the West Riding which to southerners is a foreign land.

The door opened. In came a young Staff Captain in his shirt sleeves, looked round the room, walked straight over to me, held out a hand and said, 'Hello Hodges, I'll take you first.' This was Charlie Brewer, later of the BBC. He had been my first schoolboy friend at Glyngarth, an excellent preparatory school — now extinct — at Cheltenham, to which I'd gone before I came to Bedford. He was the son of Sir Herbert Brewer, organist at Gloucester Cathedral.

We crossed the passage and shut the door. He said, 'Do you really want to come into the RFC?' I said, 'Yes, if you think I can be of any use.'

He said, 'Right! I know all about your hideous past, I needn't ask you any questions. When I've seen all these other blighters, we'll have lunch together. But we want your weight and we haven't got a weighing machine. There's one on the station platform. Will you go down to the station and weigh yourself and come back and tell me the result?'

Down I went. As I stood on the weighing machine a train rumbled in behind me. I heard loud cries, apparently a demonstration of some kind. I turned round.

In the train, just opposite, was about a score of Turkish officers. They had been the garrison of Kunfida, a town on the Red Sea. Besieged by the Arabs, after a long resistance and sick and hungry, they had to choose between surrendering to the Arabs and surrendering to the RN. They chose the RN. A camp was hastily constructed opposite Suez. Port Tewfik is the seafront of Suez, and facing it is a shallow bay, full of fierce crabs. According to local tradition this is the spot at which Moses crossed with his Jews, with the Egyptian pursuers behind them. On the rising ground above this bay we kept these brave men, the garrison of Kunfida, for a fortnight, in quarantine. Now, with an escort commanded by a brother officer, they were on their way to a big prisoners' camp near Cairo. I had been to see them every day, accompanied by a Greek interpreter named Theodore (gift of God) whom I'd never felt to be a gift of God. They had spotted me, hailed me, thrust upon me bunches of grapes and other gifts of fruit. There was much shaking of hands, which possibly surprised some of the onlookers. These were brave men who had put up a magnificent resistance. They had only done their duty, as I was trying to do mine. In a sanely governed world we should all be doing something creative. I much enjoyed this friendly demonstration and did not care a damn what anyone might think about it.

For the time being we all returned to our units. One day there was a call for a medical report, especially on eyes. Our beloved M.O. Searle said, 'I haven't got any eye-testing apparatus out here in the desert. Do you really want to go to the RFC?' 'Yes,' I said. 'Well, I've known you for over 18 months and I've never seen you walk into anything yet. I'll say you are OK.' In fact I had worn glasses for reading since I was 15, but I had never worn them on service.

One day when I was in the orderly room at Kubri Railhead, a post out in the Sinai desert, a signal came through from Ismalia. Out of those selected, twelve were to be sent home immediately for training in England, without waiting for the formation of the flying school in Egypt. Would I like to be one of the twelve? An immediate answer was wanted. I had privately decided that by volunteering for the RFC I had signed my own death warrant. If I stayed in Egypt, in all probability I should never see my own people again. If I accepted this offer I should get a free trip along the Mediterranean at the government's expense and I should almost certainly get a spot of home leave. I accepted.

What a delightful trip that was! I had no duties, no responsibilities. There was a short stay at the base camp at Sidi-Bish, outside Alexandria, teas and ices at Groppis – the famous tea-room, the inevitable shopping for presents to bring home.

The ship had on it a battalion of the West India Regiment. Black sergeants came up to me with questions which I could not answer. Just before we reached Marseilles the chap with whom I shared a cabin said, 'Didn't you know you've got a double on board? Let's go on deck and find him.' We went up, and he pointed out one of the West Indian officers. I thought he looked revolting. Evidently we have no idea what we really look like. The image we see in a mirror must be quite different from what other people see.

The trip from Marseilles to Havre lasted twenty-four hours. It was a prolonged picnic. After summer in the desert, how wonderful it was to see grapes on railway embankments! This was my first sight of France and I lost my heart. From time to time the train was put into a siding for anything up to two hours and we could wander off to a farm and eat an omelette. As this was not a corridor train, we became adept in the use of buffers for private purposes. You had to make your way along the outside of the train, hanging on to door handles. With one foot on the plate on top of the buffer, the other on a similar plate over the coupling, one hand reaching up to hold onto one of the steps leading to the roof, there was one hand left free for essential duties. With the train streaking up the Rhone valley this could be quite exciting.

After a fortnight at home I was ordered to join a school at Oxford. When not in lecture rooms we were in the Park, and I found myself looking at a big solid red brick house, 16 Park Road, at the window of a bedroom in which, as a very little boy, I had been bathed in a tin tub in front of a gasfire. This had been the last home of my grandfather, my mother's father. How astonished he would have been by these unseemly goings-on in the Park, which looked so peaceful from his windows. There was a big flight of steps up to the front door, and the diningroom on one side and the drawingroom on the other were high above the level of the road and had a fine view down the park. A great thrill had been the sight of a man, probably an undergraduate, driving two fine chestnuts tandem in a dogcart, with a well-trained Dalmatian running under the dogcart, between the wheels.

Below the drawingroom was the breakfastroom. No-one ever had breakfast in it, but it contained things which delighted me. There was a landscape with a church tower and a windmill. If the necessary winding had been done, the clock in the tower told the time and the sails of the windmill turned. There was a painting of a Victorian girl with fair hair and very blue eyes and ribbons. If you took a pace to the left, the girl disappeared: in her place was a gay bunch of flowers. A pace to the right — there was a ship in full sail. I used to reach up to put my little hand in grandpa's big hand. He was tall, handsome and very gentle. He loved trees. He took me into his beloved park and showed me the bark of the various trees. I think I owe my love of trees to him. I know nothing about them, I'm no botanist – I love them for their beauty. It was here that I was allowed to go for my first walk alone, on condition that I did not cross the road. Off I went, feeling very, very brave and adventurous up to the corner, along part of Banbury Road, across which I could see St Giles' Church. On Sunday morning Granny took me there. When the gentlemen came in they sat on the edges of their pews and prayed into their top hats. This interested me, for at home in our country church no-one had a top hat. Then along by St Giles. In those days that great space was quite empty and peaceful, and you could walk about it as safely as if you were in a field. Then a turn to the left, along Keble Road and so back into Parks Road.

It was exciting, when mother and granny went shopping in the market hall. Along past the Museum we went, past Wadham. At one point there was a delightful glimpse into a great garden. Was it Trinity? Then the Broad. Even at that age I was excited by the dome of the Radcliffe Camera. Little did I think that I should one day have rooms in a building designed by the same man, the great Gibbs. Father hoped I would one day go to Oxford and was at first pained when I went to Cambridge. But when I was offered a closed exhibition at Cambridge I accepted it at once, for I knew father had no money. Meanwhile he took me for long walks, telling me lovingly the history of Oxford.

In 1916 I was billeted in Jesus. It was there that the news came to me that my friend Denniston had been killed in France.

We spent much time rigging, which in those days involved the very precise adjustment of all the cross-wires between the two planes of the biplanes, which were B.E.2cs. In the park we started up engines by swinging props, taking great care to fall away backwards, with hands well clear, when the engines suddenly started. We did no flying, for at that time all the ground training was done first.

Among the twelve who had come from Egypt was a little

man who looked like a laughing gnome. Heseltine. He was already a qualified observer. We had struck up a friendship and intended to apply for the same squadron. One day we went for a good walk, down Mesopotamia, through Marston and Wood Eaton, down the hill and over the bridge to Islip. This was my mother's birthplace. How familiar all this was to me, although I had not seen it for nearly twenty years. Mother always had a photograph of Islip Bridge in her bedroom. We passed the old vicarage, and I thought of the oak-panelled dining-room. Then we went down to the present vicarage, the house in which my mother was born, in which as a child I had been the guest of my uncle. For a child the garden was a place of delight.

With two years behind me I was a veteran and, although still a subaltern, was the senior Lieutenant in the school. This position gave me one duty. Every morning early I paraded a party of officers in the Broad, took them at the double down the Turl, across the High, which then had no traffic, down to the Broad Walk. There someone else took them over for physical jerks, after which I took them back to the Broad.

One day towards the end of 1916 there was a call for volunteers for balloons. I had never even heard of observation balloons. Apparently they had been found useful during the battle of the Somme, and more were wanted. Sticking to my principle, I volunteered. Heseltine was furious — I had let him down. I pointed out that if he too volunteered for balloons we should still be together. But he would not. We were to meet again after the war.

2. Learning the Elements

The Balloon Depot was at Roehampton in the grounds of the Roehampton Club. I was billeted in East Sheen in a road between the Upper Richmond Road and the Thames. The family consisted of the mother — a widow, two daughters and a son. The daughters lived at home and went up to the city every day. I do not remember having seen the son. He was employed in the Mint and on that account was exempted from military service.

On our training timetable time was found for the history of ballooning. We learned of the importance of the brothers Montgolfier, of Annonay, about 40 miles from Lyon, who in 1783 inflated a linen globe of 105 feet in circumference over a fire fed with small bundles of chopped straw. It rose to a great height and after ten minutes came down about 1½ miles away.

I remember fire-balloons, without passengers, as the *piece de resistance*, the grand climax at the end of village schooltreats in our Derbyshire world. At Long Lane, north-west of Derby, in which remote place I was born, a ha-ha or sunken fence separated the field from the lawn on the south side of the vicarage. When the time had come for tired young people to end their games and go home — and home might be up to two miles away — father opened out a red and white paper balloon under which, on a light wire framework, was a wad of cottonwool.

This was soaked in methylated spirit. A match was applied. The balloon was held carefully until it obviously had a good lift and was eager to be off. Then it was released and away it went into the heavens, getting smaller and smaller, sailing away downwind, a romantic link with the unknown world, with infinity, an expression of our childhood's yearnings.

At the moment of release a kind of sigh of ecstasy issued from our little hearts, a modest forerunner of that great sigh that rises from Trafalgar Square when the great Norwegian Christmas tree bursts into brilliant light. Can it be that my joy over these simple fire balloons was the seed which was to grow into a great love for balloons? I do not think anyone can be neutral about balloons. In that respect they resemble deserts — you hate them or you love them. I had been happy in the desert, the desert with no machines in it but infinite space and silence. I took to ballooning like a duck to water.

There were to be occasional lapses. Are we not told that the course of true love never runs smooth? Well do I remember a day in Flanders, on which I was walking alone up the lane leading to the balloon field. Bitterly did I ask myself why on earth I had ever left my regiment and come to this horrible show. I felt an acute desire to turn round and walk rapidly in the opposite direction. But once I was in the air all fears disappeared. I felt happy, exhilarated, even at the most hectic moments.

One moment of doubt came very soon. I was taken up by an instructor for a short spell so that I might familiarise myself with the balloon-basket and that he might observe my reactions. In fact I was alarmed by the apparent frailty of everything. The steel cable which linked us to the winch had a diameter less than that of the nail of my little finger. All the lines seemed strangely frail. The basket only came up to my waist. How fragile the basket seemed! Though the floor was strengthened externally with wooden battens, it gave under our feet. Before long I was to have complete confidence in that steel cable and in all the rigging and was to realise that the basket so combined strength with flexibility that it could survive brutally violent treatment.

Feeling scared, but hoping I was succeeding in concealing the fact, I looked out over Barnes Common towards Hammersmith and to the left away towards Richmond Park, the great curves of the Thames and the rows of suburban roofs. In those days there were no civilian air services. To be in the air was an adventure.

But let me return to the lecture-room and continue our history. The experiment of the Montgolfier brothers attracted so much attention that a fund was raised in Paris, and a balloon was constructed by two brothers Robert, under the super-intendence of the physicist J.A.C. Charles who proposed the use of hydrogen. The balloon was of thin silk varnished with a solution of elastic gum, about 13 feet in diameter.

Inflation began on August 23rd 1783 in the Place des Victoires. The crowd was so great that on the 26th the balloon was moved secretly by night to the Champs de Mars, about two miles away. Next day, about 5 o'clock, a gun was fired and the balloon rose very rapidly to about 3000 feet, unchecked by a shower of rain which drenched to the skin the spectators, including many ladies. About three-quarters of an hour later it fell in a field near Gonesse about 15 miles away and was torn to shreds by the terrified peasants.

On September 19th 1783 Joseph Montgolfier repeated the Annonay experiment at Versailles before the King, Queen, court and a host of spectators. Inflation lasted 11 minutes. The balloon rose to about 1500 feet, came down after eight minutes in the wood of Vaucresson, about two miles away. In a cage below the balloon were placed a sheep, a cock and a duck. They were none the worse except that the cock had a wing damaged, but this was because the sheep had kicked it.

On October 15th 1783 Jean Francois Pilatre de Rozier (1756-85), a native of Metz, superintendent of the National History collections of Louis XVI, ascended in a captive fire-balloon, took up fuel and fed the fire, which was in a brazier suspended beneath the balloon.

On November 21st 1783 Pilatre de Rozier and the Marquis d'Alardes first trusted themselves to a free fire-balloon, from the Jardin du Chateau de la Muette, in the Bois de Bologne. It rose to about 3000 feet and descended about 9000 yards away, having been in the air 20 to 25 minutes. Ten days later, on December 1st 1783, J.A.C. Charles ascended from Paris in a balloon inflated with hydrogen. It was constructed by the brothers Robert, one of whom went up with Charles. It was 27 feet in diameter. The car was suspended from a hoop fastened to a net. It rose from the Tuileries to about 2000 feet and came down at Nesle, 27 miles from Paris about two hours later. Robert left the car and Charles went on.

In November 1783 Count Francesco Zambecarri, an Italian who happened to be in London, made a balloon of oiled silk, 10 feet in diameter. Filled with hydrogen and launched from the Artillery Ground, it came down 2½ hours later at Petworth, 48 miles from London.

On February 22nd 1784, a balloon 5 feet in diameter and filled with hydrogen was let up from Sandwich in Kent, and came down at Warrnton in Flanders, 75 miles away. This was the first balloon to cross the Channel.

The most important part of our training at Roehampton was a series of trips in free balloons, the good old round ones. A captive balloon might easily become free, if, for example, its cable was cut by a shell or a fragment of shell. If the occupant had not been trained, the result would be a crash and death. The training is really very simple, but if you have not had it, you are helpless. It is like riding a pushbike. Either you can or you can't.

Until recently balloons have appeared in advertisements for all kinds of things, from soap to motorcycles. Nearly always they are wrongly portrayed. They are made pear-shaped, but they should be spherical. When a free balloon leaves the ground it is not full. If it were, there would be an immediate loss of gas as soon as the balloon began to rise, for as the balloon rises the gas expands. Before the balloon ascends, the gas, thrusting upwards, fills out the top half forming a dome which, by means of the net in which it has been placed, supports the weight of the basket and its contents. The lower half of the balloon can and should be quite floppy. As the balloon is spherical, there will be a roughly equal thrust in every direction. When the gas has completely filled the balloon, if it continues to expand some must escape, otherwise the balloon would burst. This is quite simply provided for in a way which is foolproof. From the bottom of the balloon hangs an open tube, known as the sleeve. As the expanding gas cannot find any other way out, it forces its way down this tube and some escapes.

For training purposes we used coal gas. If a balloon was rising fast one could sometimes smell the escaping gas. There were people who allowed passengers to smoke. To me this seemed very unwise. The risk might be small, but it was real. A man has the right to give his life for a good cause, in fact it may be his duty to do so; he has no right to throw it away stupidly and to endanger others.

The net ends in lines which, by means of boxwood toggles are made fast to a wooden ring. From the underside of this ring substantial lines come down to the corners of the basket and, if the basket is a big one, to intermediate points. When the net is freed from the ring it can be drawn off the empty balloon, which can then be packed into the canvas bag carried about for the purpose. The balloon then looks rather like a very large pudding ready to be boiled. It is wider than the double doors of a luggage van, but can be forced through by the pushing of vigorous porters, acquiring a waist in the process. Ballast is carried in thirty-pound sandbags. The sand should be slightly damp. If quite dry it behaves as dust and might get into people's eyes, or otherwise be a nuisance. If too damp, it would cake and be dangerous. Ballast released in the air is quickly dissipated and no-one down below knows anything about it. Bags can be carried on the outside of the basket, but so far as I can remember we always, or nearly always, had ours inside the basket on the floor. A trowel is provided with which to shovel out ballast.

An aneroid barometer is provided to indicate height. Unfortunately barometers do not work fast enough to tell you at once whether you are going up or down, and there are times at which it is important to know this. A second instrument was carried, a statometer. It looked like the barometer, but was larger. From its lower side hung an open rubber tube. If you pinched this tube between your thumb and forefinger, the needle swung round the dial, telling you at once whether you were going up or down, and more or less how fast. Only one of the statometers in the store was working, and there was keen competition among pupils drawing stores to get hold of the one that worked. The instructors did not seem to worry in the least. I soon saw why. Each carried a packet of cigarette papers. If you unfold a cigarette paper, lay it flat on the palm of your hand, then launch it carefully over the side, you can see at once whether you are going up or down.

There was a trail-rope, 120 feet long, coiled on the outside of the basket, held fast by a line. Soon after starting you cut the line, the rope uncoils and hangs vertically. You now have an automatic shock-absorber. The nearer you come to the ground, the greater is the length of rope on the ground, and the weight of the rope which is on the ground is no longer hanging from the balloon and pulling it downwards.

At the end of quite a short rope is a grapnel. On a long rope it would be dangerous. As it is, if you are coming into a field over a hedge, you drop the grapnel just as you are about to cross the hedge and it will hold.

Looking around the basket we have forgotten the balloon itself. From the basket to the balloon run two lines which are very important indeed. The first is the valve line.

Obviously we cannot control the balloon's movement laterally. Where the wind goes the balloon goes. A balloon has no air-speed. We can control it vertically either by putting out ballast or by releasing gas. As gas is always thrusting upwards, the obvious place for the gas-valve is at the highest point of the balloon. There a circular disc is held firmly against the inner side of a seating by springs made fast to an arch across the opening. A simple arrangement of levers at right-angles to one another has the effect that the valve disc can rise and fall vertically but cannot be displaced sideways. From the underside of the valve a line goes straight down through the balloon, through the sleeve, to the basket. The pilot has a direct vertical pull against the springs. When he has let out some gas and releases the valve cord, at once springs bring the valve up against the seating with a 'plonk', which can be heard clearly for it is magnified by the arc formed by the top half of the balloon. If the pilot heard no 'plonk', he would know that his valve had stuck open.

I have only once heard of this happening. The chap concerned suddenly thought, 'I heard no "plonk".' He tried again. No audible result. He tried several times. Still no result. Here he was, with the valve stuck open. This meant certain death. In an agony of agitation he flung himself about in a wild dance of despair. In the end, one of his violent jerks did the trick. The valve shut with a 'plonk'. He had let out more gas than he had meant to. This could be remedied by putting out some ballast, but sooner or later he would have to let out some gas in order to come down and land. What would happen then? He didn't spend a happy afternoon – would it be his last on earth? In the end he decided that if he had to die he might as well get it over. The valve worked, and he did not die. The trouble was due to the carelessness of a storeman who had issued a valve which had not been used for a long time. It had been on a top shelf and a thick layer of dust had settled on it. The dust had combined with the oil to form a sticky paste.

The remaining line is the rip-cord. The balloon envelope is made of several layers of finest quality Egyptian cotton, impregnated with rubber. It is quite substantial and by no means flimsy. The fabric is cut in sections like those of an orange. Sometimes, when landing, it is necessary to have some means of stopping a balloon dead. If the rip-cord is pulled, the balloon ceases to be a balloon. In an instant it loses all its gas. How is this done?

In one of the panels there is a permanent slit starting just below the valve-seating and ending just above the equator. This slit has its edges reinforced with stitching and fabric, as if it were an immense button-hole. Inside this a patch is fixed, held by stitches and rubber solution. To the top edge a line is made fast and taken across to a toggle, where it is held by a light line. Now it is taken across to a second toggle, this time with a lot of slack, and there made fast. Now it is taken down through a special little aluminium hole of its own on the underside of the balloon to the basket. There the pilot, if he is wise, makes it fast in his own corner of the basket above his head, in such a manner that no passenger can possibly get hold of it. All the other lines are the colour that ropes usually are. This one is bright red. All the other lines are round. This one is a flat tape so that even in the dark a man knows if he has the rip-cord in his hand. If the pilot wants to rip, he gives a sharp jerk. A lot of slack falls through into his hand. He gives a second jerk. Only a very little slack comes through this time. Now there's nothing between him and the rip. When he judges that the moment has come, he reaches as far up the rip-cord as he can, then brings his right hand down to his feet. Now he no longer has a balloon.

Obviously one must not rip too soon, nor too late. Normally, if you rip when the basket is level with the treetops of elms in Southern England, you will reach the ground as the balloon collapses. I have ripped once and found it a very satisfying experience. Of that, more later.

We were shown a mobile gas-making plant. Into one end a certain quantity of water was put; into the other end, silicon. The result was hydrogen and a most caustic sludge. In fact, overseas our hydrogen was always delivered in steel cylinders.

My first instructional flight started from the Wandsworth gasworks. In those days gasometers were more often than not surrounded by pillars which ended in sharp spikes. If therefore you started from a confined space between gasometers, as we did, the balloon had to have such a lift that it would shoot up above the gasometers before the wind could catch it onto a spike. Our balloon had such a lift. The unfortunate ground-crew were putting every ounce into it, as if practising for a tug-of-war, panting away as if their hearts would burst.

There were four of us, the instructor and three pupils. I was told to take charge of the maps, someone else was told to keep a log. What the third chap was to do, if anything, I cannot now remember. Perhaps he was just a fag, a putter-out of ballast. The wind was blowing from the North, very gently. Just above us was cloud. I knew nothing at all of England south of the

Thames. I got out a map and started looking for useful landmarks. The ground-crew were using a device known as a spider. A number of handling guys were led into one point and spliced together and into a metal end which finished up in a U. Into the U fitted a plate, which in turn was the end of a short line on the basket. Through U and plate went a pin, with a lanyard on it. A jerk on the lanyard would pull out the pin and there would no longer be any connection between the ground-crew and the balloon. I was studying a map, aware of the pantings of the ground-crew. Suddenly there was complete silence. I looked up from the map and was astonished to find we were already well above the gasometers. The ground-crew had all sat down heavily.

We disappeared into cloud. In course of time we came out of this clammy coldness into bright warm sunshine. What had looked so gloomy from below now looked white and clean from above. How warm the late autumn sun was up here! This was really splendid. In course of time we lunched, revelling in the sunshine. Then I began to think it might be a good idea to go down and see where we had got to. How, otherwise, could we keep a log? The wind might have changed. In fact it had changed, not in direction but in speed, from about 4 to nearer 40. The others agreed. We dropped heavy hints. The pilot was not impressed — he was enjoying the sun. We went on dropping hints. At last he gave way and started down, but this was not so easy.

A warm, buoyant balloon, trying to get into a dense cold mass is like a cork bobbing about on a pond. He kept his valve open. At last we sank into the cloud. Now we were in a cold, clammy mass and lost all our nice warm buoyancy. We now had less gas than we should have for this height. He still kept his valve open. We came out of the cloud at about 2000. Ahead of us we saw the sea and the outskirts of Brighton, but we still had about six miles to play with. But the pilot never let go of that valve-line. We went down faster and faster. Very naughtily I threw out a paper-bag with a banana skin inside it. To my amazement it shot upwards. I found this demoralising. We must be going down at a terrific speed. The earth was rushing up. At last something happened. The pilot shouted, 'Bend your knees!' I bent mine — I was lucky, for at the moment we struck I was facing backwards. I had a good grip on two lines coming down from the ring to the basket.

We hit the ground very hard indeed. I felt as though all my joints had somehow come unstuck. Then there was an uncanny silence. The other three seemed to have disappeared. My corner of the basket, which had been vertical, now appeared to be horizontal. Still holding tightly to my ropes, I was looking up into the sky. What had happened? I pulled myself up to look over the side. About sixty feet down a ploughed field was whisking past so fast that the furrows were all blurred. We'd bounced.

I just had time to think 'We're going to do it again!' Then we struck again, this time at the base of a thick old hedge. The basket was crushed. Someone came hurtling round the basket like a billiard ball, flung his arms round me and held on. Now I had to support his weight as well as my own. Turning my head, I saw the smooth turf of the downs skimming by just under my left shoulder. I forced my head forward and up and pulled us both up as close as I could to the upper side — if I relaxed my grip we should both have our necks broken.

The pilot now reappeared. He had intended to rip but, when we first struck, he had lost his grip on the rip-cord. Now he was trampling about on the third pupil, trying to recover the rip-cord. In the end he did so, and ripped. We crawled out and sat in a row, feeling very sorry for ourselves. There were no broken bones. I felt very addled and no doubt the others did too.

The pilot said, 'I'm going to get my cap.' Now, when we first struck, I'd lost my cap, so I got up to go with him and we set off together. I felt an urge to make it plain that I was not demoralised by these goings-on.

I said, 'I suppose this is quite a normal landing.'

He was not pleased. He evidently thought his leg was being pulled. Was it? I've sometimes wondered. I really was feeling very addled, and I did want to impress my instructor. But the Almighty has given me a perverse sense of humour which has an awkward knack of cropping up just at the wrong moment. But I think that time I was innocent. A moment later I realised he would have to go on alone, for I had a most violent pain in my left ankle. There was no bone broken, but a severe sprain.

We had covered about three-quarters of a mile trailing over the smooth turf of the Downs before he finally stopped us. All this, seen against the skyline, must have looked very dramatic to the inhabitants of the lovely little village we could see below, with its great barns. The whole population was streaming up towards us. First came the boys, then the policeman, then the older folk. They seemed a little disappointed. There were no corpses.

They gave us willing help in packing the balloon. This is always welcome, but on this occasion we could not have done without it or at least the pilot would have had to do all the work. Of the other two pupils, one had a kink in his back — he just could not stand straight. After that day I don't think I ever saw him again. Presumably he gave up ballooning and possibly had to leave the army. I can only hope the poor chap did not have that dreadful twist for the rest of his life. The other fellow had had both his thumbs put out.

On these instructional flights the man in charge was given a certain sum in silver with which to reward those who helped to pack the balloon. It was not enough, and we supplemented it from our own pockets. When the packing was finished, whoever was in charge made a little speech, thanking those who had packed, explaining that it was not possible to reward everyone personally. Then, with the magnificent gesture of a grandee distributing largesse, he flung a handful of silver into the air and they all scrambled for it eagerly on the ground.

For packing the net, disconnected at the ring, is drawn off the balloon. The valve is removed. The empty envelope is laid out flat. Then two teams start rolling it in from both sides towards the centre. Then the balloon is forced into its canvas bag.

Just outside the village, in a cosy thatched cottage, lived an artist. He invited us to tea. Very pleasant it was, after such strange happenings, to enjoy tea and lots of buttered toast before a fire of flaming logs, surrounded by the paintings of our host. Then, with the balloon on a Sussex waggon, with a mighty horse in front of us, we went slowly on our way to, I think, Horsham — or was it Lewes?

Here I was given the telegrams and told to take charge. One telegram was sent off at once, to say when and where we had landed. At Victoria — or was it Waterloo? I can never keep them sorted out, I so very seldom travel south of London — a porter came running up. When I said I had a balloon in the guard's van he looked at me as though he thought I was tight. I had to be firm and explain we should want more than one porter.

When we had got it out, he asked what we were going to do with it. When I said, 'We'll put it in the cloakroom,' he again looked at me dubiously. Then I sent off the second telegram to the depot, to say where the balloon was. It would be collected, the rip-panel would be made good and the balloon would be ready for use the next day.

Having got back to Roehampton we sought out the MO, who lived somewhere off the Upper Richmond Road. He bandaged us up. Now we were back in the Upper Richmond Road. It was dark, black-out was complete and it was foggy. I asked a constable to stop a bus. Bus after bus came along but, though he talked to us quite amiably, he made no attempt to stop one. This seemed odd. Looking at the constable I realised what was going on in his mind. With my sprained ankle I was walking oddly, the second one of the party could not stand straight and the third, holding up his hands with his thumbs sticking out all over the place, said, 'We've been ballooning — we've left the balloon in the cloakroom at Waterloo.'

The constable thought we were all tight. In the end I stopped a bus myself. No sooner were we settled than the man with the thumbs held up his hands, looked round the bus and proclaimed loudly, 'We've been ballooning. We've left the balloon in the cloakroom at Waterloo.' Then everyone in the bus thought we were tight.

The next morning I made my slow and painful way to the Orderly Room, to tell the Adjutant the doctor had said I must have a fortnight's leave. An ankle was sprained and, as we

A general view of the Great Balloon Race, Hurlingham, 1900.

Checking the rigging for the Great Balloon Race, 1900.

Models of captive balloons in the Aeronautical Museum, Meudon, France.

crashed through the old hedge, I had had a violent biff in the back. The Adjutant then said that if I had really had a sprained ankle, I could not possibly have endured the long walk to the Orderly Room. This detonated me. I made it plain that if he didn't apologise at once for this insult I should have to stay there till the Commanding Officer arrived and tell him what had taken place. He apologised.

Now I thought of mother with her house and her parish cares, never resting, in a house three quarters of a mile from the village. Rather sadly I wired to my Aunt Fanny at Windermere to ask if she could take charge of a sprained ankle. Then off from Euston to Windermere and there followed a heavenly fortnight in the dear house, Broad Oaks, high up on the road, which runs from Troutbeck Bridge, up through Troutbeck village to the Kirkstone Pass, with its view right down the length of Windermere and across the head of the lake to the Langdales and Coniston Old Man and Weatherlam. From the little WC at the back there was a view up the valley, with Ill Bell and High Street on the right. Below the garden there were the woods and the beck.

In the evenings there would be a fire in the great music room, with its oak panelling and its barrel-vaulted ceiling, its delicate plasterwork, with bands of high-relief, oak-leaves, bramble, local themes. Uncle Charles sat down at his Bechstein and played sometimes his own compositions but more often his beloved Bach, and on Sunday evenings, hearts heavy with thoughts of our many friends who had been killed, and of Cousin John who had only recently been killed in a flying accident over his own aerodrome just outside Birmingham, we sang, 'For all the saints, who from their labours rest.' The moderns will scoff — well, let them scoff!

3. Further Instruction in England

My next trip was with a very different instructor, no less a person than Pollock who had won the Gordon-Bennett race before the war, landing far away in Russia. This was indeed an honour for us. In a balloon-race the object is to get as far as possible. To do this, the pilot is extremely economical, both with gas and with ballast. He strikes a balance as soon as he can, and keeps it, watching for movements up or down and checking them.

It was said that Pollock, I think in this great race, was over the North Sea when a passenger, who was new to ballooning, said he wanted to relieve himself. Pollock told him he couldn't. Some time later the passenger said he must, no matter what the effect on the race might be. Pollock then produced a bottle and told him to make use of it, so keeping the weight in the basket. This may be legend. From what I saw of Pollock I should say it is probably true. He was a very sensible person.

Our flight with Pollock was on a Saturday afternoon. This was most unusual. Normally there was no ballooning on Saturdays. There might be lectures in the morning, but Saturday afternoons were free. However, the balloon had been prepared for some reason or other, and we were detailed to make use of it. One of the pupils was very disgusted because he had arranged to meet his girl. Pollock heard him lamenting. He was a good sort. An instructional trip could not last less than an hour. Pollock promised that he would drop this chap as soon as he could and then go on to complete the trip with the rest of us. The log would contain no reference to the fact that a passenger had been dropped and had not completed the course. Pollock promised to keep his mouth shut if we did. We were to see what a really great balloonist can do.

As soon as we were at last clear of houses Pollock said, 'I'm going to put you out in that field,' and pointed to a field which was being ploughed. It looked impossible. The field was relatively narrow, much longer than it was broad. The two long sides were bounded by continuous lines of tall elms. Our line of flight would take us straight across the narrow width of the field, across the two lines of elms.

Pollock came down fast at a steep angle. He cut it so fine that I thought he would crash into the top of an elm. He didn't. He just missed it. Meanwhile he had said to the one to be dropped, 'Sit on the edge of the basket with your legs outside. When I say, "Jump", jump at once. Don't hesitate!'

He had so placed himself that if the passenger hesitated, he, Pollock, could give him a biff in the back. We just missed the elms, coming down very steeply. When we were about 15 feet from the ground Pollock said, 'Jump' and the fellow jumped. He landed on all fours on the freshly ploughed earth. We just touched, for a moment the rigging slackened, then, the balloon, freed from the weight of 10 or 11 stone, shot up like a rocket just missing the second row of elms. The discarded passenger was now on his feet, waving to us.

At the far end of the field the ploughman was turning his horses. His face was worth seeing. A few moments before he had been ploughing in a field which was empty except for himself and his horses. Now there was a man in the middle of it and a large balloon leaving it.

We completed our hour. Presently we saw we were about to pass over a very extensive park. The long stone house was very large. Everything looked well maintained. Surely there would be plenty of gardeners and footmen to lend a hand with the balloon. We dropped hints to Pollock. He was not interested. A little later we saw a railway line. Pollock dived into one of the pockets in the lining of the basket, produced an ABC timetable and told someone to see when the next train left Billericay. This was a place in Essex whose name had become widely known because a Zeppelin had been shot down there. Pointing to a field ahead he said, 'I shall land there,' and he did. He came down hard. With memories of the Sussex downs still fresh in my mind I did not feel very happy as I saw the earth coming up.

We had to pack the balloon ourselves. Somewhere we found a farm. Then came once again the delightful ride on a farm wagon behind a mighty horse. There was just time for a welcome cup of tea and we were off from Billericay. We asked Pollock why he had not landed in the park which had seemed a much more suitable place. He said, 'I once landed there and they didn't even offer me a cup of tea.'

In the pre-1914 England the great country houses had been in the same hands for a long time. The old hands amongst the balloonists knew their hospitality standards; they knew whether they could expect a cup of tea, dinner, even a bed for the night or the weekend, and they landed accordingly. Socially Pollock was very respectable — his brother was Solicitor-General.

There was one colourful instructor with whom I was never privileged to go up. He used to leave his pupils in the basket, climb up the net and sit up at the top where he could work the valve with his hand. He once left London in the afternoon with a wind taking them more or less north-west. Darkness fell, he carried on. Suddenly they crashed through a wood. There would be no real danger in this. A line ran round the inside of the rim of the basket so that one could hold on without getting knuckles damaged, as they would be if they protruded from the basket. In case things got really hectic, there was a similar line down near the floor. You could hang on and brace your feet against the opposite side. Even if the basket was upside-down you would still be safe!

They had hit the top of the Wrekin in Shropshire. On they went. Suddenly they heard a strange murmuring. Fortunately the chap in charge had the sense to realise this must be the sea. Down they came. They landed, but at once the basket turned

over and they went out into space. They had landed at the edge
of a cliff and gone over it. Fortunately for them the tide was
out. They saved themselves and the balloon, but the next day
the pupils looked a bit sorry for themselves.

My most delightful trip was with de Ropp. I hope I have spelt
his name correctly. He could see no point in hitting the ground
hard. He thought landings should be as gentle as possible. I
agreed with him. In this life we get more than enough
bashings-about without asking for them.

On a lovely sunny autumn day we flew very low. Most of the
time the end of our trail-rope was on the ground. We kept a
good look-out ahead. If we saw a line of telephone wires or
some glasshouses coming we put out a little ballast and lifted
the rope clear. The woods were all scarlet and gold. Hares and
rabbits were frightened by the shadow of the balloon and
cowered down close to the earth.

Outside one farm was a big herd of shorthorns. We were very
low. The trail-rope was running across the back of a cow that
was lying peacefully chewing the cud. Not unnaturally the cow
wondered what was the cause of this unusual tickle and got up
to investigate. The curious action of the cow which, unlike the
horse, gets up stern first, is always somewhat undignified, even
when seen from ground level. From our moderate height we had
a full stern view, which completely concealed all the front half
of the animal. The cow took a few paces forward till the rope
dropped off her hindquarters, then about-turned and stood
gazing down at the rope making its way across the grass.

The expression of bewilderment on the face of the cow was
unbelievably funny. It was also strangely moving. I had an
uncomfortable feeling that we had been very naughty. After all,
we needn't have trailed the rope across the cow's back. We
couldn't change our direction, but we could have put out a little
ballast and lifted the rope clear.

De Ropp and the two other pupils were town-dwellers — I
was not. Brought up in South Derbyshire, since earliest
childhood I had had cows around me. Even now when at home
on leave, I looked out from my bedroom window on to cows in

fields, and on summer nights it was a delight to listen at the open window to the sound of the cows pulling at the grass as they grazed in the darkness. Cows are sociable, affectionate and highly strung. Although I had been amused, I did not feel quite happy. I wanted to make my peace with the cow — to explain things. But alas! All too often in life we cannot stop and explain.

All the afternoon the sun shone. The trees and woodlands of East Anglia were aflame with glorious colour. At last it occurred to me that we were quite a long way from home. In those parts railways seemed to be rare. I pointed out to De Ropp that there was a railway a mile or two ahead, but there would not be another one for a long time. He decided to land. We were flying parallel to a straight road, along both sides of which, just ahead, were the houses of a village. A woman crossing the village street looked up, saw us and let out a shriek. They all came running out of their houses.

De Ropp leant out and shouted, 'Come along! Come along! We're going to land over there.'

We came in over a low, well-laid hedge. As we crossed the hedge someone dropped the grapnel. We stopped, so gently that I wondered whether we were on the ground or not. I looked over the side. We were floating about four inches off the ground. A pull on the valve-line — we settled down. This seemed to me a perfect landing.

The valve was held open till the balloon collapsed. There had been no need to rip. The balloon would be returned to store intact. As usual, the villagers were eager to help with the packing. A farm cart was found and off we went to the station. I cannot remember where this was. It was far away beyond Cambridge and we should have to change trains at Cambridge. The thought of being on the Cambridge platform was too much for me. I suggested to De Ropp that the other two pupils should toss up to decide which of them should take the balloon back to London. Then he and the other pupil could dine with me, if possible in King's.

As soon as we got there I dashed off to the kitchen to ask if they could produce three dinners. They could and did, in rooms in Gibb's though not my own. What a day! For hours we had been floating over East Anglia, exulting in its gold and flaming autumn beauty. Now we dined before a fire, in this eighteenth century room with its cream panelling, its tall, perfectly proportioned windows, the absent owner's pictures, in the peace of King's. I thought of the hours I had spent poring over Gibb's book of designs in the College library, when I should have been devoting myself to the synoptic gospels.

Early in my teens, if not before, my father had taught me to love Gothic building. But he had been ordained deacon in St Paul's and priest in St James' Piccadilly, and very early he had given me a book on Wren. All through my boyhood I had longed to see some multi-millionaire build somewhere the cathedral Wren had wanted to build, the cathedral of the model. Having seen Gibb's design in his own book I had looked with new eyes at All Saints, Derby.

I could not then foresee that one day I should live in Paris, should become acquainted with the too self-conscious Invalides, the noble Val-de-Grace, the delicate beauty of the Grand Trianon, that I should spend months in Munich, that I should live in Hamburg and become acquainted with the Michaeliskirche, that with Swiss friends I should visit the great church of Einsiedeln and the lovely chapel of Ittingen.

Over long years a slow change was going to take place in me, till in the end I should come to feel that Baroque was restful and satisfying and Gothic was too often restless and somehow fussy, with the exception of Perpendicular, peculiar to England. Even as a boy I had felt that the round arches of the Normans were nobler than the points of the Gothic builders. Gloucester I knew, and Ely. Durham, as noble as any, I was not to know till late in life.

Between Long Lane where I was born, and Derby, there was a farmhouse — the Wheathills — which had a fine old drawing-room. In the long wall of this room was an oval alcove. When as children we sometimes played in this room, this alcove fascinated me. Though I could not have put the thought into words, obscurely I was realising that there can be no really satisfying beauty without curves. There were curves in the trees, in the lovely grasses, in the leaves, in the flowers, in the violets in the mossy banks, in the roses in the garden and the lovely wild roses in the hedges, in the sweetsmelling hawthorn, in the primroses, in the bluebells, in the Lords and Ladies, in the apples and pears and plums, in the raspberry canes, in the chestnuts, in the long scarlet-runners and in the broad beans too, even in the little radishes. There were curves in horses, in the great Shires and the splendid mounts of the Meynell Hunt, in the cattle, even in the mighty pigs, in the geese and in the ducks.

In spite of good company there were sad thoughts. Buchanan was dead, hit in the head by a stray bullet in Gallipoli. Northampton friends too had gone, all in Gallipoli. I did not really believe I should survive the war. Meanwhile here, for a short space of time, there was peace, the peace of King's, a fire, good company and Audit Ale.

A day came on which I must go up alone with an instructor and do everything for myself. He would just watch me. Of course, he would not wish to be killed and if he saw I was going to do something very silly he would butt in. We started off towards the Essex countryside. It was a sunny day with a lot of patchy cloud. When the sun shone on the balloon we became buoyant and went up; when a cloud obscured the sun, we sank again. These varying conditions very nearly proved my undoing. When we had been up for over an hour I suggested we might land. Just ahead was a suitable perfectly flat field. Unfortunately I forgot to look upwards at that moment. As we came in nicely over the hedge, the cloud which had obscured it uncovered the sun and the sun warmed us up.

Instead of settling down, the balloon became buoyant and tried to take off again. Though I held the valve open continuously the sun was gaining on me. We went down the fortunately big field in a series of long hops. I realised that the next hop but one would take us straight into a big elm-tree in the hedge at the end of the field. It was, of course, the only tree in the neighbourhood. If our line of flight had varied ever so slightly to left or right, we should have missed it and we should have had a succession of level fields to play with. I could, of course, have dumped thirty pounds of ballast and risen over the tree. The balloon would have cleared it. If the basket didn't and got mixed up with the top branches, it wouldn't have mattered. It would have crashed through and got clear.

We used to be told that if, by some misfortune, the trail-rope took a hitch round a chimney, even a factory chimney, there would be no need to worry. All you had to do was just to hang on. The pull of a balloon is tremendous. Sooner or later the chimney would go. Naturally this would not make the balloonist popular either with the owner of the chimney or with the higher command of the RFC, but that is just an occupational risk. Now that there are so many miles of high voltage transmission lines running about all over the place, it would obviously be wise to fly at a height, which would keep the trail-ropes clear of everything.

The tree was straight ahead. Another hop and a half and we should be in it. An immediate decision was necessary. Turning to the instructor I said, 'May I rip?' He said, 'Yes.' I ripped. We stopped dead, just short of the tree.

I have retained an exact photographic recollection of other trips, of what people said and what people did. But at this point my mind goes blank. Is this a result of excitement over the rip? Presumably we packed the balloon alone. How did we get it to the station, and to what station? It was somewhere in the country out beyond Acton and Hanwell. In the end we must have come to Liverpool Street — of that too I have no recollection at all.

Now came the real solo. We went up from Hurlingham. There was a polo-ground there, but the club also catered before the war for duchesses and distinguished people who wanted to make balloon ascents. The club had a private gas main from the gasworks across the road.

There were about half-a-dozen of us. I was the second starter. Before I was ready, No. 1, a Naval officer, was well away. I had a small solo balloon, borrowed from the RNAS (Royal Naval Air Service). I went away with a splendid lift, clearing the trees easily and, looking round for landmarks, saw the West Brompton Cemetery.

Then I disappeared into a fog. Here I was till further notice, in a fog over London. It is forbidden to land in London. I could hear the traffic down below. As long as I heard that, I should know I was still over London. I have already said that the army coiled the trail-rope on the outside of the basket. Perhaps because they are accustomed to coiling ropes on decks, the naval people didn't do this. They coiled the rope on the floor of the basket. The basket of a solo balloon is already small. When a rope has been coiled in it there is not much room left for the pilot. When I stood on my coil, the side of the basket barely reached up to my knees.

I sat down on the coil and gazed out into space, feeling like an airborne Buddha. However, I could not spend the day imitating Buddha. I must get rid of this rope. I flung it out. Then I looked out to see the result and to my horror saw that it was not hanging straight. Down towards the bottom were two large loops. This wouldn't do at all. Had someone been careless in the coiling of the rope? There are all manner of booby traps waiting for a man hovering over London in a fog. What if I took a hitch round Nelson?

I should have to haul that accursed rope back again. Now I have never been one of those beefy, athletic people. I have never tried weight-lifting. Still, that rope would have to come back. Moreover, once you've started hauling in a rope, you cannot leave off to do something else, however urgent the something else may be. The balloon seemed to have settled down quite nicely. She seemed likely to keep on quite steadily for some time to come. I would have to take the risk. The weight of this trail rope was considerable. I doubt if I could have picked it up and carried it when coiled.

My one consolation was the thought that, as every foot came in, the weight still hanging below would be less. Each haul would be less severe than the preceding one. Even the second wouldn't be quite so bad as the first. I set to work. At last it was all in. Then I had to pay it out again, very carefully, taking great care that in this confined space no part of it took a hitch round an ankle or arm. At last it was all out, hanging straight. I drifted along, with the fog billowing. Always I could hear the traffic, but of course I had no idea where I was.

Fortunately there are rifts in fogs. To my joy I found myself looking down a long grassy slope with a very long, large stone building at the bottom of it. This was the garden of Buckingham Palace. What a Heaven-sent place to land in! There would be no crowd. There would be people to help to pack the balloon. With luck I might even be invited to lunch. One never knows! Then I lost my nerve. I saw myself having an extremely unpleasant interview the following morning with the colonel or some more senior person. Regretfully I faded away into the fog.

Much later I saw the spikes of St Pancras, but in between there happened something strange and alarming. Looking ahead, I suddenly saw the man who had started before me, like a great orange, seen through a rift in the fog.

As I was looking at him, he suddenly fell like a stone. Now I was very much on the alert. When I reached the same spot, I too fell. We had been taught always to be very economical with gas and ballast. I put out a handful of ballast. No result. Then several handfuls. No result. I took the trowel and put out a trowelful. No result. This was quite abnormal. Out went several trowelfuls. No result. Rules no longer applied. I seized a sandbag, upended it and shot out the lot, 30 lbs. No result. Another one, making 60 lbs. No result.

I was now below 150 feet and falling fast. My knees were trembling. There was just time for one more. Out went another, making 90 lbs. The balloon checked and very slowly began to rise. I was now very low. I thought, 'At least with luck I may be able to see where I am.'

Below was a very large stone building with a glass dome in the middle of it. It was the reading room of the British Museum. I had very nearly landed in it. It would certainly have been an unforgettable moment.

All the afternoon I drifted, listening to traffic. At last I decided I must put an end to this. The day was coming to an end. I had not enough ballast left to allow a safe margin for landing in case I had to change my mind at the last moment. I unbuckled my Sam Browne and unbuttoned my tunic, in case I should want to throw them overboard. I was just damned well going to land, no matter where it might be. I crept down, very, very carefully. Suddenly there was a line of trees below me. The fog was so thick that from the level of the tree-tops I could not see the ground.

Seeing a straight line of trees, I stupidly called out, 'Is that the Embankment?'

A voice said, 'No!'

I said, 'What is it?'

The voice said, 'East London Cemetery, Plaistow.'

I said, 'Righto! Hang on please, and pull me down.'

The gravediggers pulled on the trail-rope; I pulled on the valve line. I settled down in the cemetery without breaking a tombstone. What marvellous luck! The wise cemetery-keeper, not wishing to have half London in his cemetery, had dashed to his gates and locked them. Nevertheless a large number of people had got in somehow. In no time a policeman appeared.

In those days I weighed only nine stone. If you remove nine stone from a balloon basket, the balloon will take off more or less like a rocket. I had to stay there, holding the valve open, till the balloon collapsed. With a crowd all round, gazing at me, I felt like a monkey at the zoo. Everyone was very cheery. One old dame said, 'Aye, I bet it gev yer a turn!'

At last the balloon collapsed. There were plenty of eager helpers for the packing. I did the noble gesture with the largesse. The cemetery keeper's comely daughter appeared and said her father had sent her to ask me if I would like a cup of tea in his lodge. I asked the policeman if he would be so kind as to stand by the balloon for a bit. Of course he would. Off I went to the lodge, made use of the telephone and enjoyed a lovely cup of tea in front of a splendid fire. In course of time a lorry appeared, took the balloon on board and off we went on the long drive through the fog to Roehampton.

Then I went off to my billet in East Sheen. I went upstairs for a wash before supper. As I stepped off the bottom step of the stairs into the hall, the front door opened and in came the elder daughter.

She rushed at me and said, 'Some of your balloon people are absolutely outrageous. Today as I was going out to lunch, one of them came down quite low and poured out sand all over the place; absolutely ruined my new hat. Look!'

I looked. Sure enough, mixed up with her rosebuds was some of my sand. Seeing the fury of this female I felt that discretion was the better part of valour.

Basely I replied, 'I quite agree with you. I hope someone reports him and he gets it in the neck.'

I never let on that I was the culprit. Though amused, I felt some disdain. If this woman had reflected for a moment she must have realised that the man concerned was pouring out sand because he was trying to extricate himself from a situation of no little danger. There were eight million people in London at that time.

Normal training in free. balloons was all done by daylight. Fortunately a few of us had an opportunity to enjoy a flight by night. One of the joys of ballooning is its silence. This seems to be intensified by darkness. Three balloons had been filled for an exercise with searchlight units. At a period in which such marvels as radar were unknown, the searchlights would have to search in the sky for these quite silent objects. Three balloons went up. The first was to fly at 1000 feet, the second at 2000 feet, the third at 3000 feet. I was in the second balloon.

As soon as we started, if not sooner, a fog came down. Rising through it, at about 750 feet, we came out into a glorious starlit night, the top of the fog looking like a level floor of pure white cottonwool, spreading on all sides to the remote horizon. At 2000 feet we found ourselves travelling on exactly the same line as the balloon at 1000 feet, but much faster. We passed over them, looking down onto them and soon left them behind. The balloon flying at 3000 feet went off at right-angles. I heard it said that someone one night went up much higher, and found himself over Hampstead. He came down lower and was brought back to Roehampton. He amused himself repeating this manoeuvre several times.

The sound of trains came up clearly through the fog, as did

the occasional bark of a dog. At the very moment when we were preparing to land, a rectangle of light appeared slap in front of us — someone's bedroom window. Hastily we dumped thirty pounds of sand and rose over his roof, trailing our rope amongst his chimneys. He must have wondered what was the meaning of the very strange noises on his roof. And what, I wonder, did he make of the heap of sand on his lawn? We had taken care neither to speak nor to laugh. When we were well away, we all exploded. Evidently we had had the bad luck to hit upon a house on a hill.

We tried again, very carefully. This time, at the very last moment, when we really had committed ourselves, a large haystack appeared. We just missed it and landed in a field of cabbages. If we had gone past the other end of the stack we should have landed in a pond. The fog was not quite so thick here. At the far end of the cabbage rows was a hedge, and beyond it, on what must be a road, what looked like the light of a pushbike.

I stumbled up the field to the hedge and haled the owner of the light — 'Where are we?' He leapt on his bike and pedalled away like a madman. Evidently he thought the enemy had arrived.

We searched round about the haystack and found a farm. They were just going to bed, but the whole family came down, stoked up the fire, made tea, put a ham on the table and we had a splendid meal in the night, surrounded by beaming faces. With the balloon on a cart behind the usual plodding hefty horse we were soon on our way to Maidenhead.

Having done a night flight I was now eligible to apply to the Royal Aero Club for an Aeronaut's Certificate, and did so. It is before me now, bearing the number 193. It is dated September 24th 1918, and the stamped portrait shows me in the new uniform of the RAF. Why had I not applied for this certificate in 1916 or, if I had, why was it not issued until 1918? I don't know.

There were two Advanced Balloon Schools, one at Larkhill, the other at Lydd. I went to Lydd and my stay there was very short. Reinforcements were needed in Flanders, and two of us were whisked away almost at once, after a brief embarkation leave.

The Orderly Officer at Lydd had one unwelcome duty. Early in the morning, before dawn, he collected from the orderly room a little instrument for measuring the speed of the wind, and the key of the church. He went to the church, let himself in, climbed up the steep winding stair in the corner turret of the tower and out onto the roof, held the instrument above the battlements — a chilly business — noted the reading, returned to the orderly room, rang up the Gunner HQ and told them the wind speed.

At Christmas everyone went home on leave, leaving two bachelor officers behind to do the duties of the Orderly Officer, and also the Adjutant who was left in command of the station. On Boxing Day morning the Adjutant announced that he was going off to spend the day shooting with some friends in the neighbourhood. Taking advantage of his absence, we two pupils now behaved improperly. We knew that sometime we must spend a whole hour at least up in a captive balloon. Why not do it today, instead of just wasting a day? We told the Flight Sergeant to put the balloon up. Moreover, once up, we told him he could dismiss the men until lunchtime. The men scattered about the countryside. At first all was well. The local hunt had a meet almost beneath us, and we were able to watch the progress of the hunt. The wind increased in force and became gusty.

Our balloon was of the old Drachen type, of German origin. It was like a huge sausage with parallel sides, with one single air-filled rudder on the underside at the stern. These balloons could be very unsteady in a gusty wind. A captive balloon has no net. The rigging is made fast to a rigging-band, with strengthening bands over the balloon. The strength of the rigging is really amazing — from that morning onwards I had complete confidence in it.

As gusts struck it, the balloon rolled violently, imparting a sudden jerk, now to one side, now to the other, through the rigging to the basket. The balloon flies as a kite, with the tail slightly down. An extra special gust would send her up, soaring kite-wise. At times a gust would strike the nose, forcing it down. Then the wind, rushing over the balloon, would produce a negative kiting action and the balloon would dive three or four hundred feet.

It was most alarming suddenly to feel the basket falling away beneath one's feet. The first time it happened I thought for a moment we would go the whole way down and crash. But the balloon recovered and there came another yet more anxious moment, when it had come back to its proper height, lifting the steel cable and, still having an upward momentum, which the cable could no longer follow, threw a strain on the rigging. There is, in fact, a relatively weak breaking-point provided, just above the head of the cable, so that if a balloon does break away it will go away with all the rigging complete.

My companion was a very steady Scotsman, who normally was in the Forestry Service in Malay. One day, someone who had a grievance against him was felling a tree on a hillside. He waited till the Scotsman was passing below, then gave the last stroke. Someone else saw the tree coming and shouted a warning. The Scotsman ran, but he just did not quite make it. He saved his life, but one arm was caught and was permanently twisted.

For the first and last time I was revoltingly sick. In December 1915, when I was coming home from Lemnos on the Mauretania, running as a hospital ship, we had terrible weather in the Bay of Biscay. Her screws were repeatedly out of the water. There were only four officer patients who could appear on deck. I was one of them. Ever since then I had thought I was proof against seasickness.

This Drachen balloon had beaten me. The Lydd landscape consisted of large rectangular fields divided by dykes. These were whirling around forming and reforming compositions very much like some modern paintings, which I am not able to admire as much as some other people appear to, possibly because they recall memories of airsickness. I became incapable of speech and had to hand the phone to the Scotsman. In any case, there was nothing we could usefully say apart from telling the winchman to let us up or haul us down. There would be no

A Drachen kite balloon nearing ground level on being hauled down. Note motor-winch on right and men hauling on ropes. A communication trench can be seen on the right.

A Belgian detachment with a Drachen kite balloon in Flanders, late 1914. Nearby the British detachment had spherical observation balloons.

point in hauling down, for until the end of the morning there would be no crew to handle us. We were neatly and fittingly punished for our naughtiness. With the Adjutant absent and ourselves in the air, there was no officer at all on the ground.

We had to endure our misery for the whole morning. At least we had demonstrated that we could survive, not for one hour only, but for several, in a Drachen balloon, in the worst possible wind conditions.

Perhaps it was for this reason that when a day or two later reinforcements were wanted for balloon units in Flanders, we two were packed off before we had finished our course — in fact, almost before we had begun it.

4. New Friendships

Ah, love, let us be true
To one another! for the world, which seems
To lie before us like a land of dreams,
So various, so beautiful, so new,
Hath really neither joy, nor love, nor light,
Nor certitude, nor peace, nor help for pain;
And we are here as on a darkling plain
Swept with confused alarms of struggle and flight,
Where ignorant armies clash by night.

Matthew Arnold

At Boulogne I came down to breakfast. There were six of us around the table, two on each side, one at each end. I was at one end. Each of us was given a sealed envelope. I opened mine, then said, 'Does anyone know anything about the Second Balloon Wing?' 'Why?' said the man facing me. 'Because I'm posted to it.' 'You poor devil!' 'Why?' 'Because the man in command is the biggest swine in the army.'

Very soon I was to find that the supposed swine was devoted to his duty and expected everyone around him to be equally devoted. His wing was devoted to him and he watched over us like a father. How often was it to happen, after a particularly trying day, that I would find the Colonel's car down below and the Colonel would say, 'Hodges, I think you'd better come and dine with us at the Wing.' In their snug little mess one could enjoy a little peace, at least a change of setting, and the consciousness of kindly goodwill in the background. His name was MacNeece.

I was to take a train, which in course of time would land me at the little country station of Castres. It was well on in the morning when I got there. The RTO (Railway Transport Officer) said, 'There's no-one to meet you yet. There's a pretty little village at the top of the hill. If I were you, I'd walk up and have a look at it.' I did. I can see it now, the first French (or was it Belgian) village I had seen, except from a train window. It was just a few farms grouped around a very old church.

When I got back there was an RFC Crossley tender in the station yard. Now we were bowling along through the country-side of Northern France, with which I was to become so familiar, which I soon learned to love and which I still remember with mingled affection and horror.

The Wing HQ was on Mont Rouge, a little isolated hill behind the villages of Locre and Dranoutre, a very much smaller hill than Mont Kemmel, or Kemmel Hill, which lay nearer to the lines – in fact one might say in them. The Colonel had a little office, so did the Adjutant, and there was a cosy little mess. From the windows or from the wooden platform outside there was a splendid view over the countryside. They had a telescope too, but this was really only a toy, a relic of early ballooning days. It was soon found that telescopes were useless in a balloon basket. We used 6 magnification prismatic binoculars with separately adjustable eyepieces. Having quickly found the correct setting for my very indifferent left eye, whenever I climbed into a basket I had only to pick up binoculars and twiddle them round to the correct setting.

At this point, as I enter a new life, it may be pardonable if I indulge in a little meditation. First, a word in praise of Army administration. Since I had left my unit, the 4th Northamptons in the Sinai desert, these things had happened. I went to Suez and there was a room for me in a hotel there. The next morning there was a place in a train, which in due course of time disgorged me at Alexandria. There was transport waiting to take me to a base-camp at Sidi-Bish. After some days I was conveyed with my kit to the docks and found a berth waiting for me on a ship proceeding to Marseilles. From there to Havre I shared an ancient 1st class carriage with three others, so that we each had a corner and could sleep, sitting, in reasonable comfort. There was a boat to take us from Havre to, presumably, Southampton. I had orders to report on arrival in London to a certain room in the curved building facing Blackfriars Bridge, known then, I believe, as Adastral House. I was, of course, expected. I was sent home and told to await orders. A fortnight later I was ordered to report at Oxford. There was a room waiting for me in Jesus College. When I moved to the balloon depot at Roehampton, there was a billet for me at East Sheen. Then came a move to Lydd, followed by embarkation leave. I had orders, at the end of the leave, to report to a certain room in London. There I was ordered to join a certain train, which connected with a boat, to land me in Boulogne, where a room was waiting for me in a hotel. At breakfast I was handed an envelope. In it were orders as to what train I was to catch in order to reach Castres. At Castres, a remote country station, an RFC Crossley picked me up and took me to the HQ of the 2nd Balloon Wing.

To me this seemed impressive, and it still does. Could any travel bureau have done better than this? In the twenties it seemed to be the fashion to laugh at the Army. I never could understand why. To me in Gallipoli, in Egypt, in fact everywhere I had been, it had seemed remarkably efficient and, on the whole, very, very noble. From the moment I first joined the Northamptons I had found real kindness, helpfulness, thoughtfulness. I was to find the same atmosphere in this wing.

After I had met the Colonel, the Adjutant and the Equipment Officer and had had a meal with them, I was shown the lie of the land and told I was to go to No 25 Balloon Section, commanded by Higman. The Wing was divided up into Companies and each Company at first contained two Sections. As Sections later became more numerous, the number in each Company increased, at least down at our southern end, for we were on the right wing of the 2nd Army. The 2nd Wing covered the front of the 2nd Army, and the 2nd Army covered Belgium from the North Sea down to the French frontier.

I had been very happy with my regiment. Now I was going to

love this wing with a fierce love. I was going to grow to love the army, for which I already had a great affection, with such a love that I should want to stay with it as a regular officer.

At the same time I should have burned into me a feeling of the most profound horror, as I looked down day after day at this utter desolation, this band of just nothing at all, nothing, absolutely nothing, which reached right across Belgium and France, right down to the Swiss frontier. We worked normally at something under 5000 feet. From the height one can see quite a long way round the curvature of the earth. The band of desolation went on and on and on, a seemingly endless ribbon of a kind of obscene porridge, with bits of man mixed up with it, no tree, no bush, no trace of track or path, nothing; nothing at all — nothing. To this desolation I was to add. If one gave oneself up to one's job, it was technically very satisfying. The direction of a successful shoot from overhead gives one great satisfaction, especially if one has destroyed a battery which has been making a nuisance of itself.

It may well be asked: 'If what you saw filled you with horror, how could you think of becoming a professional soldier?' The answer is simple, 'Soldiers do not make wars. They endure them. In their sufferings they pay the price of the errors of statesmen, who themselves are no worse than the amorphous mass of fiercely patriotic people and just unthinking people.'

Already in Gallipoli I had begun to distinguish very clearly between soldiers and politicians, between people on the spot and the people in London. Many years later I was to read Beaverbrook's book on Lloyd George. What a picture it gives us of the political world of the time! The philosopher statesman Balfour, who had written a book on the Ultimate Basis of Theism, expressed a desire to turn the Turk out of Europe. He had, of course, never himself seen a war at first hand. If he had done, he would never have spoken lightly of turning anyone out of anywhere.

One reason why I in the end resolved to stay in the Army was that I felt I had gone too far down the road to turn back. Between the Suvla front and the Anzac area there was a Hill 60, which was as evil in its way as the notorious Flanders one.

There had been fierce fighting for this crest which was an advanced position thrust out into No-Man's-Land, occupying captured Turk trenches. It was organised as a garrison with two battalions, one in the line, one in the gully immediately behind. The left and right companies enfiladed No-Man's-Land. The centre sector was seven yards from the Turks at one end and thirteen at the other. There was no wire in between. The whole area was covered with corpses, which just lay there and disintegrated in the great heat.

On our first night on this hill, for some reason or other I was taken away from my own company which was on the right and put in command of the centre company. I had someone else's company, the survivors of an Irish regiment, some Australians, some Hampshire machine-gunners and a wonderful new toy — a trench mortar. All I could do was to get round and see everybody and speak to everybody. I sat and chatted to two Australians in a trench seven yards from the Turks.

At the right of this sector, where the line bent away, was an empty fire-bay which continued the old Turkish line, then a sandbag barricade, then a bit of trench with plenty of corpses in it, then a second barricade, then Turk trench.

I went into this empty bay. I had a feeling that something was stirring, that something was about to happen. I got up onto the fire-step. It was a very dark night. Nevertheless it was foolish, for we were on the skyline. I stood absolutely motionless, hoping no-one would notice me, gazing into the blackness, listening intently. Someone threw a grenade at me. It just missed my left ear. It lay now on the trench floor between me and the only way out.

It is extraordinary how quickly you can move when you've really got to. I had to step backwards and downwards off the fire-step, turn left, do a standing long-jump over the damned grenade and get around the traverse, before the grenade went off. As I shot around the traverse, it went off.

Unfortunately an Australian had lain down at that point on the floor of the trench to get some sleep. As I came round the corner at the maximum possible speed, I tripped over his feet. One of my feet came down on some portion of his stomach, the other somewhere on his head. There are moments in life at which it is obviously better not to stop and explain. In any case, a man going flat out can't stop. I heard loud, horrific oaths rising up into the night sky.

I went to the trench-mortar people, gave them the target, went back to observe. A loud bang, but no apparent result. We repeated this. Still no apparent result. We would try once more. This time there were terrible groans. They lasted a long time.

Though I was too occupied that night, I think it was from that moment that I felt I could not come home and take Holy Orders. Listening to those horrible groans, I could not escape the fact that I had killed a man. The fact that he was a Mohammedan did not make any difference at all. He was my brother, one of the children of God. I had killed him.

What I should do after the war, assuming that I survived, which at the time looked extremely unlikely, I had no idea. Meanwhile here I was in Flanders, seeing war from a very different angle.

25 Section was not far away from Wing HQ, behind the road from Locre to Dranoutre, in a field beside a little lane which ran through a small wood in which was the balloon-bed. It was a new unit. Till the spring they would have no balloon of their own. They shared the balloon of No 2 Section, a very senior section, whose camp was next door, in the wood.

The commander of 25 was Higman, a big chap, a model of devotion and efficiency. In peacetime he had been in charge of the telephone and telegraph system of a big South American railway. His job was not being kept open for him. He had thrown it all up to come home and serve, as had so many other people. There was Whitfeld, an Australian, who had come over with the Australian Light Horse. He afterwards took an Oxford degree, married a charming Englishwoman and settled in England. I had the honour of being godfather to his son and a very bad one too.

Wilkie was a big, good natured chap whose speciality was concert parties. One day, when he had been called to the telephone to speak to the Wing, we were astonished to hear him say breezily, 'Well, I'm the Archbishop of Canterbury.' Asked to explain he said, 'The fellow at the Wing said he was the Assistant-Chaplain General, so I said I was the Archbishop.' It really was the Assistant-Chaplain General, who was interesting himself in welfare work and especially in concert parties.

The weather for some weeks was very bad indeed. It was a cruel winter. For weeks on end an icy east or north-east wind was blowing across from Russia and Germany to us. Our huts were flimsy and we lined them with newspaper. We all four slept in a little hut with a stove in it. Whitfeld and Wilkie went to bed early after supper. Higman and I huddled over the little stove in the mess-hut, in all our flying clothes, except for the long boots. I read *The Times*, he read Spanish novels. The cold was shocking. One morning there were twelve degrees of frost inside the chart-room, though there was a stove in it. Yet we were in comparative luxury. In pyjamas, enveloped in blankets on a camp-bed, with a little stove a few feet away, I felt ashamed as I thought of what the infantrymen were suffering. Every morning the bodies of men who had died from exposure were being brought out of the line.

One afternoon I was up with Nelson who commanded No 2 Section. The visibility was poor, nothing was stirring anywhere. Both sides had but one thought — to escape from this killing icy wind. No guns were firing. Everywhere was snow and silence. It was our turn to stay up and keep cave, to let everyone else know if conditions should improve. The icy wind blowing straight into our faces made us weep. Our tears froze on the lenses of our binoculars. We cleaned the lenses and started again. We wept again, cleaned again, and so on. At intervals Nelson spoke to Wing, pointing out what a farce this was. The answer was always the same: 'Someone's got to stay up there in case things improve. It's your turn. You'll have to stay up till sunset.'

At last Nelson said, 'I'll promise to keep my mouth shut if you will. Down there they can't see which way we are facing. We'll just face the other way.'

We did. For the rest of the afternoon we turned our backs on the enemy. There was no more weeping, no more lens-cleaning.

Below was snow and silence. What men were enduring in the snow below did not bear thinking about.

Very soon after my arrival Higman very kindly said to me, 'I'm going down this evening to dine with the Commander of No 2 Company down south of Nieppe. Why not come with me? It'll be a chance for you to see something of the lie of the land and to get to know the people down there.'

It was a moonlit night. We followed the last possible road southwards, parallel to the lines, through Neuve Eglise and Nieppe. Is there anything sadder in the world than a village that has been shattered by war? There were no roofs left in Neuve Eglise, and many walls were down. Jagged gables stood out against the sky. These abandoned shells had been the homes of families. In these days so many, many people live in flats. They move frequently. Can a man love a flat? Does the word 'home' ever have the same meaning for a town-dweller that it has, or had, for those of us who were brought up in the country? I have often wondered.

To me these little shattered villages were more heartrending than the damaged cities. In Gallipoli war had been a grim game in a grim setting. Even there I had been conscious both of the futility and of the grandeur of man. In the Sinai desert there had been no destruction, for the simple reason that there was nothing to destroy. When Higman took me for this drive in the moonlight, I had not yet seen this world from above, had not yet become acquainted with that horrible band of desolation across Belgium and France. These little shattered villages, seen at close quarters, were more intimately moving.

In France, to the South, the 1st Army was delivering an attack, preceded by prolonged bombardment. For several nights we could feel the pulsations of this mighty cannonade conveyed to us in the ground. Then, and later, I used to think of the untold thousands that these bombardments cost, of the houses or hospitals that might have been built. A bad soldier? No, I don't think so. This war had got to be won. I was doing my duty, and technically I found my new job interesting and satisfying.

I had a much wider view of war than an infantryman could

ever have. From the air, from somewhere short of 5000 feet, one saw an enormous stretch of country. On the ground I gradually got to know our neighbours to north and south. The time would come when I should make direct contact with IXth Corps HQ at Bailleul. At any time they could speak to us in the air. But even in the air there were days on which our minds were not fully occupied, on which one could let one's thoughts dwell upon the unutterable sadness of what we were looking at down below.

In the early days it struck me as odd that, except on days when I was Orderly Officer, I really had nothing to do and nobody seemed to worry about it. Only very much later did it occur to me that possibly there had been method in this technique, that perhaps the newcomer was being watched. The plane people provided us with fine air photographs, with vertical shots, especially of likely target areas, and with oblique wide-spreading views, taken more or less from the viewpoint of the balloon. The two together were most informative. It occurred to me that the oblique views, which covered a great depth of country, would be much more useful if they bore the lines of the grid printed on the map. I spent hours in the chart-room, working with a mapping pen, patiently transferring the grid to the oblique views, which is not as easy as it sounds.

The weather continued to be impossible for air work. I did not want to spend all my days in the chart-room. Occasionally I managed to escape. Someone offered to show me round the Kemmel area. There were two tunnels in Kemmel Hill. One really was a tunnel. At intervals a few steps led up to an O.P. We joined the gunners in one. I peered out through an aperture in a steel plate in the direction of Wytschcaete. The upper tunnel was really only a deep trench, with only camouflage cover overhead. When it came to an end we clambered out.

Facing us was a notice fastened to a tree-trunk. 'Warning. Danger of Death beyond this point.' My companion said, 'Would you like to see some more?' I said, 'Yes, please.' He said, 'Follow me, but don't join me till I beckon to you.'

He slipped from tree to tree. I followed one tree behind. At last he stopped and beckoned. I joined him. He said, 'If you put your head round the right side of this tree carefully, you'll see them.' I did so. I was looking down into a German trench, taking it partly in enfilade. The mail had come in. They were reading their letters.

One day Whitfeld and I got permission to go off for a long walk to visit a battery of field-guns, which was just behind the last ridge to the left of Ploegsteert Wood, the famous Plugstreet. To get there we followed the road till it was just about to enter the wood of ill-repute. A track ran off to the left at right-angles. From this there was access to the little farm in which they lived. It and the gun-pits nestled under the shelter of the ridge, the far side of which was exposed to enemy fire. These gunners had a very lonely life, as gunners often did. They did not share the cruel hardships of the infantry. But they had to live with their guns. They could not walk forwards onto the skyline, for obvious reasons. If they went out towards the road they would lose the protection of the ridge and be exposed to whatever might come over. The battery was cunningly sited. There they had to stay put, week after week. Rations and ammunition would come up at night.

They were delighted to see visitors. They gave us lunch. Then they put on a shoot and asked if we would like to go into the gun-pits. For the first and last time in my life I found myself in a gun-pit with a gun-crew in action. This was a great excitement. I soon began to understand why gunners love their guns. Presently the sergeant said, 'Would you like to fire the gun, Sir?' I couldn't really say 'No!', though in fact I was scared stiff. On this particular gun the lanyard which should be pulled to move the firing lever was missing. I should have to put my hand on the lever itself. I did so, taking the precautions that a man takes with the starting handle of a car. I had no wish to have my thumb shattered.

I pulled gently. Nothing happened. I pulled a bit more. Nothing happened. The sergeant said, 'Give it a good pull, Sir!' I did. There was a mighty crash. The gun had disappeared. It was somewhere down below my right elbow, beginning to slide noiselessly back again to its normal position. A beautiful, fascinating toy. Evil, but fascinating.

Then came the long trudge home. It was dark when we still had a couple of miles to go. We felt we must rest our feet and sat down on a convenient heap beside the road. It slowly dawned on our weary selves that the neighbourhood was a bit smelly, though it was much too dark for us to see if we were near a farm. We were sitting on a manure heap.

Great stress was laid on the importance of close liaison between the gunners and those who observed for them. At times a balloon-officer might be attached to a battery for a week. I never had this good fortune. All the more was I grateful for my day with the Plugstreet battery.

Whitfeld and I asked if we might do a parachute jump. The answer was, 'No! You'll have to do it some time in the next fortnight. Wait till you have to.' The parachutes we used were automatic. That is to say, if a man were thrown out unconscious he would land all right. The parachutes hung on the outside of the basket. The lead from the harness ended in a spring-hook, an enlarged version of those used on dog-leads. We snapped them on, as we got into the basket. When a man jumped, his falling weight pulled the parachute out of its case, which remained on the basket. A used parachute could be re-packed and used again. About one in a thousand did not work, although carefully packed under supervision, and no-one could ever say why. That was why MacNeece had not allowed Whitfeld and me to make a practice jump.

One day I was up with MacKay of No 2 Section. The visibility was pretty poor. Nothing was happening anywhere. Suddenly a German battery fired. The balloon-basket is hung from a trapeze and can swing fore and aft. I weighed nine stone, MacKay a great deal more. I was at the forward end. The floor of the basket was therefore permanently uphill.

When the battery fired, instead of keeping his eye on the spot MacKay became violently excited. Crying, 'Good God man, did you see that?' he leaped from his rear end of the basket to my forward end. The basket swung round the trapeze. I suddenly found myself facing face downwards towards the earth and beginning to slide out of the basket. Reaching backwards, cursing volubly, I got a grip on the lines and hung on. MacKay retired to his end of the basket and all was well again. I besought Higman never again to send me into the air with MacKay, and he did not.

It may have been that same trip that saw the end of a beloved old balloon. It had been patched more than once and the patches did not match the original fabric. It had a Heath Robinson look and was known as 'Lousy Lydia'. Old age had made it porous, and there was a plentiful mixture of air in the hydrogen. On what was to be its last day it could hardly lift us above 1000 feet. The result was furious enquiries from Wing. 'What are you doing at this absurd height, practically on the ground?'

I explained that the balloon just would not go any higher.

'Nonsense!' said the incredulous MacNeece. 'Come down and I'll go up myself.'

We were to be proved liars. We went down. The Colonel was put into a parachute harness and hitched onto a parachute. We all stood around. The command 'Let up!' was given. One end of the basket rose a foot or two from the ground. The Colonel's end remained on the ground. Lousy Lydia couldn't lift him even one foot. The old lady was dead. In a silence that could be heard, the Colonel got out and departed.

It must surely have been thanks to Lousy Lydia that three of us wangled a trip on a lorry down to Haazebrouk. In a tiny room behind a tiny shop we ate a dinner cooked for us by a beautiful and motherly woman, who showed us photographs of her fine hat shop in Lille, now behind the German lines. She was eking out an existence somehow, with her tiny little shop and restaurant. She spoke of musical evenings in her Lille home. Though she was unwilling, we selfishly persuaded her to sing, and in this tiny room, with a splendid voice she poured forth an operatic selection. I do not think any of us were particularly musical, but for a short time our thoughts were carried away to our own homes, our own mothers, away from the daily beastliness. She knew it, and that is why she sang to us, though it made her own heart ache. That evening and that kind heart I've never forgotten.

For Christmas MacKay had ordered haggis from Scotland. They arrived after Christmas and I was able to sample haggis for the first and last time. I have never wished to repeat the experiment. He sent one to the Colonel, with disastrous effects. The CO had spent some time in the East and his insides were not too good. I gathered that after he had eaten haggis, he was unapproachable for some days. He suffered from constipation. When constipated he was intolerable, at other times a most delightful man. It was always considered to be one of the Adjutant's duties to estimate daily what luck the Colonel had had and to let everyone else know. Thereby hangs a tale.

Up near Poperinghe was a section commanded by a man by name Russell. Russell was due for leave the following Monday. The days were passing. He heard nothing about it. He became uneasy. He thought he would ring up the Adjutant, who was a pal of his. He spoke from his mess. With one ear he was listening to conversation round the fire, with the other he was waiting for the Adjutant. The latter was out, or engaged. Instead of saying so, the orderly caused the Colonel to come to the telephone. Hearing a voice, Russell said, 'Hallo, you old devil! Has the Colonel had a good rear this morning?' It was the Colonel's voice that replied, 'Thank you, Russell, a beauty. How kind of you to enquire!' Russell was so demoralised that he rang off and forgot to ask about his leave.

One day the Colonel was up at Russell's section, and Higman was there too. Moreover Higman was in the air. How it came about that Higman had taken up Russell's balloon I do not know. Higman was a keen man and he may have been glad to have a chance to look at that sector. The visibility was poor. Nothing was happening. He was keeping cave at something like the full height of 5000 feet. Everyone was bored, including the Colonel. As a result of too much air-work, he had a bad stammer. It rarely happens that the air is quite still. It was still that afternoon and the balloon was flying practically over the winch. It had in fact drifted a very little.

He picked up the winch telephone and said, 'Hig-Hig-Higman, we were wondering what would happen if you dropped a sandbag.' After a pause he said, 'Hig-Hig-Higman, did you get that?' Then he said, 'Good God!' and ran like hell. Higman had answered, 'Yes Sir. It's gone.'

This stout canvas bag, with a flat bottom, containing thirty pounds of sand, went straight through a thick plank footbridge and penetrated some distance into the bed of the ditch below it.

No 2 had, in a man by name Gavin, an outstanding observer. Later on, when I had a sector of my own, I think I really knew it by heart and I do not think anyone could dig a hole or do anything worth mentioning without being spotted. It was my ambition to be as good as Gavin, or as nearly so as I could, but in one respect at least I knew I should never equal him. He had an unrivalled knowledge of the German routine, of the railways in the background. While he was still on the way up, a cheerful voice might say, 'There's a train running into Roubaix from the south. There shouldn't be.'

The bitter weather continued. We received a welcome issue of little heaters, the size and shape of the early flat pocket torches. They burnt sticks of a patent fuel which looked like charcoal. They were provided with a chain and safety-pin. They could be carried in a pocket and used as hand-warmers. I used to pin mine in the small of my back, so that there was one warm spot at the base of my spine. In spite of that, in this cruel wind that went on for weeks I used to feel quite naked, as if the wind were whistling round my skin, though I was wearing a leather flying coat, tremendous fleece-lined boots up to the thighs, a flannel-lined Burberry tunic, an oilskin waistcoat lined with flannel, a warm shirt, a camelhair vest, the warmest of pants. How must the Germans and Russians have been suffering on the Eastern front? Our own infantrymen were dying from exposure every day.

Years later, in 1962, a Swede told me that in the second war he had seen Red Cross trains crossing Sweden conveying back to Germany broken-down, blank-faced lunatic men. In Gallipoli I had been amazed by the amount of suffering and exhaustion that men can stand. Here was a new horror, the prolonged cold.

One day, one of our men, a fat man, disappeared. Presumably he had deserted. So far as I know he was never traced. Where had he got to? Where could he conceal himself? After all, we were relatively comfortable. There was a rumour that he was disaffected 'agin the war and everything else', and had possibly deserted forwards to the enemy. How could he do that? I was in a new world. With the Northamptons I had never even thought of such things. Four of us had been sent from Cambridge to bring the officers of the 4th Battalion, the Territorial battalion, up to strength. How kind they had been to us! We were taken into the family. We felt we were honorary members of the county. That had been delightful.

In this Balloon Wing I found a new delight. The officers at least were drawn from all over the Empire, and still further afield. Whitfeld had come over with the Australian light horse. Later on, in my own section, there would be a lawyer from Jamaica. The Anzacs, who had been our neighbours in Gallipoli, were now in the Second Army, and before long I should be observing for them, as also for Canadians. Here indeed one could feel the Empire was a great family. Someone has rightly said that the British Empire was the greatest of the achievements of man. It was. It was greater than the mediaeval church, though that too at its best was a noble vision. But the Empire was concerned with justice and freedom, and with the task of educating people for freedom. It was a delight to work with people from all over the earth. The men — a willing, kindly crowd — seemed to me to be largely Cockneys, or at least from counties around London, though there were notable exceptions especially among the NCOs.

The days lengthened. The cruel wind ceased. The snow had gone. Though it still had no balloon of its own, No 25 moved away from No 2 about two miles to the south. At least we could prepare a bed for the balloon that was coming. Meanwhile we took it in turns to provide a crew to handle the one balloon we had got.

The bed was prepared by clearing an area, rather larger than the balloon, in a conveniently placed wood. The ground would be levelled, or rather so shaped that any rainwater would drain into a ditch round the side. The area of the bed would be covered with canvas sheeting, so that there would be no mud,

The basket of a kite balloon, equipped with telephone, map-rest, parachute, and parachute harness. Note the trapeze above the basket. During the author's period of service, hand telephones were not used; the observer had a mouthpiece on his chest. Map-boards were not used, the maps being carried in a pocket in the basket lining. The basket was narrower, with room for one man on either side of the trapeze. Normally only one person went up, which made for efficiency and safety in the case of attack.

Aerial view over Ypres, with British trench-line in the foreground.

Aerial view of Ypres, in which the Cloth Hall can be clearly seen.

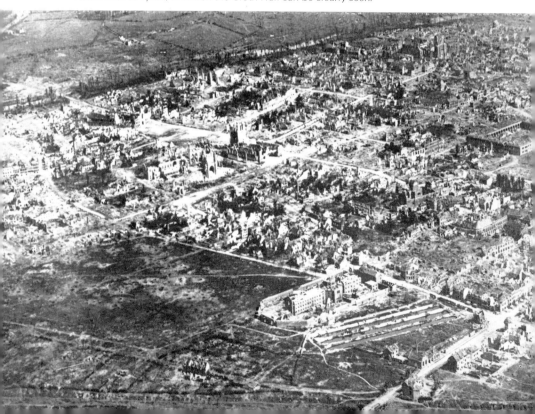

and the bed would always be clean.

I had become attached to our little camp near Locre and Dranoutre, and remember it still with a kind of Old Boy affection. The new camp was quite remote, on a country road, which led uphill to a large crucifix. In each Balloon Section one officer, known as the Balloon Officer, was personally responsible for the welfare of the balloon and the parachutes. This was my job. Every morning I set out to have a look at the balloon, for it had arrived almost as soon as we did. I went up the hill, facing the crucifix. Before I turned right, down the hill towards Bailleul, I always paused and looked up. Truly we were hacking fresh wounds in His heart every day, yet I knew I was not a pacifist. We were defending a civilisation and men's freedom. But what has all that to do with Christian teaching? I envy people who think they have found the answer to this problem. I have never done so. At the bottom of the hill I turned left, away from the Bailleul road, and very shortly came to the balloon bed, beautifully sited, cut out of a dense wood on the reverse slope of a hill. The balloon was protected against wind and against shell-fire, and there was a safe road for the winch to work on.

Down at the bottom of the hill which ran up to the crucifix there was an empty rest camp. There was no-one there at all, not even a guard. On the second evening we were there, it being a nice spring evening, the men drifted out of camp in twos and threes, strolling down the hill. The Flight Sergeant too felt an urge to go for an evening stroll. Even more strangely, one of our lorries was seen to leave the camp. The officers were all engaged elsewhere. It had been noted earlier that in the huts in the rest camp there were wooden bunks with bottoms of wire netting. In course of time everyone came back. That night every man in No 25 had a bunk — there was no more sleeping on the floor.

Such was the shortage of balloon officers that units were being ordered to detail officers for balloons. There had been a stage, at which ballooning was looked on as a soft option. That stage was long since past. People had seen balloons burning.

One lovely spring day, with the air as clear as could be I went up with a companion of whom I held no high opinion. Before long we witnessed an unpleasant drama. A German fighter came along, fleeing for his life, pursued by a British fighter. The British fighter had got the German taped. Unfortunately, instead of pressing the button and settling the matter, he was enjoying himself, creeping up a little closer to pump his bullets into the other man's back. Intent on the job in front, he did not realise that a second German was doing the same thing to him. It was horrible to have to watch this and to be quite helpless and useless. There was no way in which we could warn or help him. It was the second German, the one at the back, who fired first. The British plane fell past us, with the pilot enveloped in flames. A few seconds earlier he had been triumphant. It was not pleasant.

My companion went a most peculiar green colour. He cowered down at the bottom of the basket saying, 'For God's sake go down, man, for God's sake go down.' We were not flying at our full height. I said into the phone, 'Let up!' For a moment I thought of throwing him out, but it would have been so embarrassing for him when he landed, and he might have struggled and resisted and I should have had to hit him. I felt a kind of physical contempt. In all my infantry experience I had never seen anything resembling cowardice, or lack of self-control. It was horrible to see a man so degraded. At least, that was what I felt then. I was young, and inclined to see things in black and white. The psychologists have taught us to be more merciful, more understanding, in fact more Christian.

Although I did not think of it at the time, I have since wondered why the German fighter did not turn his attention to us. We were quite close to him, a sitting target. It may be that his attention was so completely concentrated on shooting down the British fighter and saving his comrade that he just was not aware of us.

I reported to Higman, asked — please — to be spared further trips with this fellow and suggested he really was not going to be of any use. With his usual goodness of heart the Colonel was merciful. He said the man was a beginner and had not had time yet to find his feet. Much later, in England, I heard he had been sent back to his battery. Poor devil!

5. A Fortnight in France

The First Army was attacking down south of us, in France. It was thought desirable to make some sort of demonstration on their left flank, to make the Germans think something was going to happen there too, and prevent them from moving reserves southwards. The Second Army would lend the First Army two balloons for purposes of bluff. Nos 25 and 32 would move south into France, and be for the time being under the command of Major Stringer, a cavalryman when he was not ballooning. No 25 would be looking over the area of Flers and Fromelles, No 32 would be a few miles farther south. I was told, 'There's so much moisture in the air over the valley of the Lys, the visibility will be very poor. You probably won't be able to see anything useful. That doesn't matter. The one thing that matters is that you should show yourself to the enemy as much as possible.'

With a few men I went on a day ahead to prepare the balloon bed and instal primitive sanitary arrangements. The farm we occupied had hitherto been spared by war. As was usual in those parts, the farm buildings were grouped around a yard, in the middle of which was the manure heap. The house itself, of one storey, formed the inner side away from the road. The windows of the kitchen, or livingroom, which we occupied, looked onto the court and the manure-heap. In the beams of the ceiling were hooks from which we hung our parachutes.

The next morning the section arrived and almost simultaneously an invitation from the gunners to visit their O.P. Higman went off, with Whitfeld and Wilkie, leaving my companion of the last unfortunate incident with me. I had so little confidence in him that I unwisely did not give him anything to keep him occupied. All the morning I was kept busy, keeping my eye on various tasks. It never occurred to me that it might be wise to keep an eye on him.

The morning passed. The others had not come back. He and I lunched alone. As we finished, the others came back looking a bit shaken. The gunners had taken them up very long ladders to the top of factory chimneys, from whence they peered through holes either deliberately contrived or just knocked out by a passing shell. Every man to his taste! The gunners said nothing on earth would induce them to come up in our balloons. Our people thought the gunners' chimneys were, to put it mildly, bloody awful.

Higman said, 'Put the balloon up! You may as well go up yourself. We've had a hectic morning and we want a meal.'

I told the Flight-Sergeant to put the balloon up, then I stood and watched proceedings. This Flight-Sergeant was a tough guy. For some years he had been in the Liverpool Police Force, and it was said he had an intimate knowledge of the ways of Chinatown. He certainly had always given me the impression that he had nerves of brass.

As I watched him, I felt he was not his usual self. There was something odd in his voice, his expression. He was ill at ease. I moved till I was quite close to him. Then I said, very quietly, so that no-one else could hear: 'Flight, there's something the matter. You're worried about something. Tell me what it is.'

He said, 'The front parachute there, it won't work.'

The riggers were told to take that parachute back to the house and to bring out the third one in its place. They looked astonished, as well they might.

While they were doing this the Flight-Sergeant explained: 'This morning, while we were all out, that chap was fooling about, hanging from a parachute and pulled it out of its case. He daren't tell you. He came and told me, and I pushed it back and made it look all right outside, but of course it's in a mess inside. I was hoping I'd have a chance to get it out somehow and get it properly packed.' 'Flight, if it looked all right outside, how could you know that one of the parachutes the riggers brought out was the faulty one?' He said, 'Sir, this morning when I pushed it back, I took the precaution of rubbing my muddy boot against the side of the case. Look, here's the mark. I saw that and that's why I was worried. If you hadn't spoken when you did, I should have had to do so. But of course I didn't like letting the chap down.' Good old Police Force!

I had had lunch alone with the culprit. He had had all that time to tell me what had happened. He just hadn't had the guts to do it. I should just have sent for a rigger and watched it being re-packed, so that from that moment I should have been the man responsible if anything went wrong. He had said nothing, not even when the balloon was being put up.

Every captive balloon and every non-rigid airship keeps its shape by means of a simple device. It has in effect a false or double bottom. When the balloon or ship is high or warm, the gas expands and forces the inner envelope against the outer one. On the underside of the balloon there is a scoop, facing forwards. The wind, passing over the surface of the balloon or ship, enters this scoop and forces itself into the so-called ballonet, filling the space between the two skins, if there is any space, and in any case inflating the big stern rudder which contains air, not gas.

If a balloon should break away, losing the great weight of the steel cable which is rigged below the bow of the balloon, the nose turns upwards, the balloon stands on end, the basket with its independent rigging bashes back against the rudder, and it becomes impossible to use a parachute attached to the back of the basket. For this reason, if there are two observers in the basket they are given three parachutes, two in front, one astern. The fellow at the back hitches himself onto the stern parachute. If the balloon breaks free, he can quickly unhitch himself and transfer himself to the spare front parachute.

When a balloon was struck by an incendiary bullet, at first nothing much seemed to happen. There was just what looked like a rather large gas jet burning, apparently quite steadily. Seemingly quite slowly the flame grew broader. Then suddenly, with a rush, there was flame from end to end, and the balloon was falling. Between the moment at which the balloon was struck and the moment at which it fell, there was just time for two people to leave the basket and break their parachutes free. There must be no hesitation. There was a tale that farther south someone had taken up a Brigade-Major. Almost at once, before the poor major — who had never been off the ground before — had had time to settle down and look around, they were attacked and set on fire. The balloon man said 'Jump!' but the poor major just could not face it. He hesitated. The balloon officer knocked him out and threw him overboard. Did they meet subsequently, and was there any embarrassment? There shouldn't have been, if the major was a good chap, and probably he was.

Why, between the wars, did people find it so amusing to laugh at Colonel Blimp? After all, there is something to be said for men who understand the meaning of such words as honour and loyalty, for men for whom life has not been a rat-race.

One day when Higman and I were up, it was discovered that we could move neither up nor down, thanks to an electrical fault down at the winch. To make matters worse, those below had not reported this to those above, hoping to cure the trouble before we knew anything about it. The necessary spare was not available. A replacement would have to be fetched from far away, possibly from Haazebrouk. This happened while we were on loan. What would the First Army think of our efficiency? Higman's comments were sulphurous. I almost thought I could hear the line sizzling. We'd got to get down somehow. Of course we could have parachuted, but that would have left the balloon up there, a fair target for anyone who happened to pass by.

The winch, mounted on a long chassis, was driven by its own 30 hp engine. It was not possible to turn this winch by hand. Use had to be made of a spider. A number of ropes were spliced in to one head, as in the device used by a ground crew to hold a balloon before it took off. Now, however, it led to a pulley. This was placed over the cable and the crew walked away across country until such time as the balloon reached the ground. As we started at something near 5000 feet, it took quite a long time.

Anything less dignified than this slow, diagonal descent it is difficult to imagine. Higman was incandescent. To me the whole operation seemed incredibly funny. Fortunately there were no Germans about that afternoon. If they had caught us low down, it would have been awkward, for then we should not have had room to parachute. Our luck was in.

One day I was up alone, as usual. In the Lys valley the visibility was poor and nothing was happening. Stringer was bored and impatient. About every ten minutes he rang up to ask if there was anything to report. This seemed to me fatuous. Obviously if there had been anything to report I should have reported it. I was conscious of his ill-concealed irritation. Again came the question. Again I said 'No'.

Then he said very sharply, 'It's a damned funny thing you can't see anything. For some minutes now Smith of 32 has been reporting train movement at Flers. There's shunting going on there.'

I said, 'Well, Sir, I'll watch the place for the next ten minutes and tell you the result.'

I glued my glasses on the spot. There was no train movement. There was a long silvery streak, which looked just like the smoke of an express train rushing across the country, but this streak did not move. So it could not come from a moving train. If an engine were shunting, it would not lay a flat streak of smoke. The smoke would come up in puffs here and there. What was I looking at? It had rained earlier in the day. Through the misty light I was looking at the reflection of the feeble sunlight from the wet roof of a long shed beside the sidings.

When Stringer next rang up, I explained. Poor Smith had been misled by his eagerness to satisfy an impatient man. I am sure that Stringer would be just enough to realise that. I did not at all like letting Smith down, but what else could I do? We

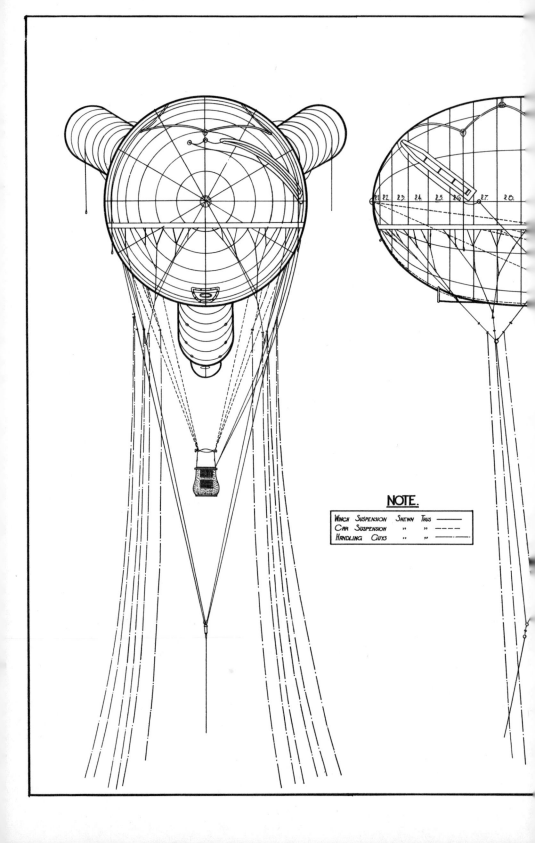

NOTE.

WINCH SUSPENSION	SHEWN	THUS	———
CAR SUSPENSION	"	"	— — —
HANDLING GUYS	"	"	—·—·—

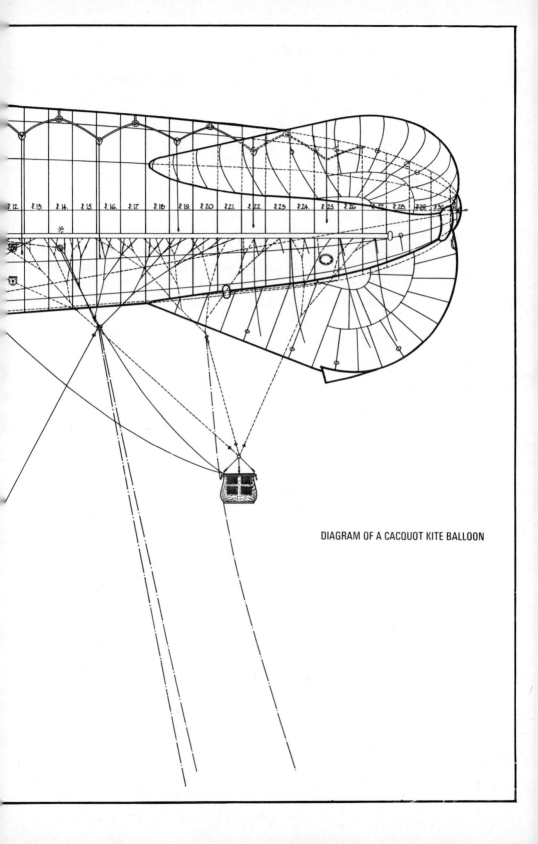

DIAGRAM OF A CACQUOT KITE BALLOON

were in the air to observe accurately and to say exactly what we had seen, neither more or less. From that moment Stringer's manner changed noticeably.

Again in the second war I worked in close contact with a cavalryman. They seemed to me a special breed, and a fine one, quick-thinking, humorous, devil-may-care, kindly and possessed of a quite remarkable richness of vocabulary. Has mechanisation changed their nature? I hope not.

Behind the farm was a big wheel in which a dog was placed every morning to walk inside the wheel and so to churn out the butter. It was a handsome young dog. Its paws were not yet deformed by this daily uphill work, but they soon would be, as could be seen in the case of older dogs. It churned for several hours every morning, then was led back to its kennel in its yard and chained up. This was its life. It never got a walk, even up the orchard. In any case, after its churning it was much too tired to do anything but lie down and wait for the next day's labour.

Someone suggested that it would be a good idea to rescue (i.e. steal) this dog before it became deformed. Everything was planned. The Flight-Sergeant would unchain it and lead it to Higman who occupied an Armstrong hut in the middle of the orchard. He would bring it to me. To be near the balloon I was sleeping in the scullery of a cottage at the far end of the orchard. I should walk with it down the lane beside the cottage. In doing this, I should have to be careful, for in places the mud was so deep that on one occasion a chap stepped right out of his gumboots and came down in his socks in the mud.

At the end of the lane a Crossley tender would be waiting for me and the dog. By side-roads we should cross from France into Belgium, back to our normal home near Crucifix Corner and hand the dog over to the guard there. Then I should return and go back to bed in my scullery. At daybreak the farmer's family would find us all asleep as usual, but the dog would be missing.

The dog would have to be on really friendly terms with us. He must really trust us. The theft would have to be postponed to nearly the end of our stay. As the dog would have to make quite a long journey with me, it was essential that he should learn to trust me. Every day I paid him frequent visits and, if he was not asleep, caressed him. On one of the first days I was stupid enough to put a hand on him just after his food had been put down before him, with the result that he bit me. Much alarmed, I dashed off to the MO. It healed quickly without any apparent after-effects. For some days after that I wore gauntlets when handling the dog, till I felt we knew one another well enough for me to take the risk again.

The great day came. No doubt the farm people suspected that something was in the wind. They all slept at the back, but they put an old farmhand to sleep in an outbuilding opening into the yard. Any sound in the yard would awaken him. Somehow he must be made harmless, but no harm must be done to him. This was the responsibility of the Flight-Sergeant, the Chinatown expert. Every evening he invited the old man to drink with him. On the appointed day they drank as usual. What did the Flight Sergeant drop into the old man's beer? He swore it was nothing but tobacco ash. The old man slept soundly that night, and all the next morning he was walking around holding his head and groaning.

I slept as usual in the cottage scullery near the balloon, ready at a moment's notice to slip into some clothes and go off down the lane with the dog. But no dog was brought to me. At one moment I thought I heard sounds coming from the orchard, but I was not even sure of that.

The dog, unchained by the Flight Sergeant, had walked with him quietly out of the yard, past the end of the house, across the orchard to the Armstrong hut. When the door of the hut was opened and the dog saw or smelt Higman, he was so excited that he let out a yelp of delight, just one. That was enough. In no time there were dancing round the hut the farmer, his wife, two daughters and a boy in his teens. The door being bolted, the boy tried to break open the celluloid windows. The Flight sent through the window first his clenched fist, then a volley of fortissimo curses. The game was up. It only remained to hand over the dog, who would be deformed and churn until he died. There were gloomy faces around the breakfast table next morning.

Our bluffing mission being over, we returned to Belgium. The balloon crew manhandled the balloon across country; stores and personnel went off in lorries and tenders. Higman gave me permission to return across country on foot. So I had the great joy of a quiet country walk across the fields. It was a beautiful spring morning. Up above a lark was singing. The peace was not complete. An enemy plane passed over. AA guns fired at it. Everything that is shot into the upper air has to come down somewhere, and it was a nose-cap that came whirring down and landed only a few yards from me.

A little later I was following a path with a good thick hedge not far above my head, and there was a deafening crash. There was a battery of 60-pounders in gun-pits beautifully concealed in this hedge. The blighters had seen me coming and had waited until I was just below the gun. Or was it just pure chance? Someone must have had a good laugh.

In spite of these interruptions I thought much about this land and its history, of which I knew so little. I made up my mind that, if possible, I must learn more about the land, the people, Picardy, this North French and Flemish world. They are so near to us, but what do we know about one another?

The Colonel very properly insisted that when we went into Bailleul, or any other town, we must be properly dressed. We must not wear any odd bits of flying clothing. Gumboots too were barred. I had a yellow pair, which were not quite so conspicuous as black ones.

One day, having got permission to slip off to Bailleul for an hour or two for necessary shopping and a little peace, I was at the foot of the steps leading up to the entrance of the officers' club, when the door opened and out came the Adjutant. At that moment I realised I was still wearing my gumboots. I had forgotten to change.

Acting on the principle that attack is the best form of defence, I said, 'I know what you are thinking. If you say anything, you'll be an absolute . . . !'

He laughed and departed. The next day, when I came in after inspecting the balloon, I was told I was wanted at the Wing. 'Had they given any reason?' 'No, they hadn't.'

This was alarming. It might well happen after an eventful or strenuous day that the Colonel would extend a welcome invitation to dine with him. No one was ever sent for during the day. It must be those accursed gumboots. I was driven up to Mont Rouge. With sinking heart I went into the little mess. By the fire sat Jones, the Equipment Officer, known as Jonah. He had been a Balloon Officer, but had gone deaf, very deaf, as Balloon Officers sometimes did, and for this reason had been made Equipment Officer.

I asked if he knew why I had been sent for. Had it anything to do with gumboots?

'Well, my dear chap,' said Jonah. 'You know how mad keen the Colonel is on this subject. If you will be such a B.F! I mean, you have fairly asked for it, haven't you? I'm damned sorry it's happened. It was a bit of bad luck. By why be such a B.F?'

I was summoned to the presence.

'Take a seat,' said the Colonel, indicating a quite comfortable chair. This was a refinement of cruelty. 'Have a cigarette.' Another refinement of cruelty.

Then he spoke. 'Hodges, Smith of 32 Section is going home to England. He needs a rest. I want you to take command of 32 Section. You'll find yourself directly facing Messines, on the curve of the salient. That will be an important sector.'

I was dumbfounded. I was almost the junior officer in the Wing. Now I was going to have a show all of my own. My own chart-room, my own telephone-exchange, my own transport, lorries, cars, motor-cycles, my own family to look after. I was going to be responsible for the happiness of all these people, with a camp all of our own. It was marvellous, too good to be true. Smith had left that morning. There was no reason why I should not leave No 25 that afternoon and go down to 32 to take over.

There was another bit of good news. Higman was leaving 25 to take command of No 2 Company. No 32 was in his Company. We should not be separated. We should be a few miles apart, but I should still be under him and we should see each other probably almost daily.

'Well,' said the Colonel, 'Good luck to you. Don't forget that

I shall always expect to see you longer in the air than anyone else, higher in the air than anyone else, and nearer to the enemy than anyone else!'

6. A Family of my Own - No. 32

I liked the look of my new family. Unfortunately, almost at
once they were naughty. An officer of the French Mission
wanted to know what action was to be taken in the matter of a
missing ladder. While 32 had been bluffing in France, they had
borrowed a longish ladder from a good woman, who, in the
absence of her husband with the army, was running her
smallholding single-handed. When 32 moved back to Belgium,
the ladder had disappeared. What about it? I could only explain
that I had just arrived, that I had not been with 32 in France,
that I would do my best to find out what had happened.

None of the three officers could remember any ladder.
The Flight-Sergeant knew nothing about a ladder. The Frenchman was regretful but firm. The ladder must be found or
he would have to report and demand compensation. With his
approval I drove into France to the little farm, very small,
where 32 had been stationed. I explained who I was and why I
had come. Fortunately the good woman understood my Higher
Certificate French. Why, by the way, do people everlastingly
produce stale jokes about 'la plume de ma tante' and school
French. People in France do in fact have both pens and aunts. I
was taught very well, both at my Cheltenham prep school and
at Bedford, though our books were not quite so attractive as
they sometimes are now.

With her I searched the farm, especially the ditches. I could see the hooks on which the ladder would normally rest. There was no sign of a ladder. Had there perhaps never been a ladder? The state of the hooks showed a ladder had been resting on them fairly recently. I was puzzled and worried. I could only assure the gentleman at the French Mission of my good faith and good intent and beg him to hold his hand just a little longer.

Days passed. Many days. We had no wood to shelter our balloon. It was surrounded by high canvas screens, supported by tall wooden poles, braced by wires. The wind sweeping across the flat fields threw a great strain on poles and wires. Some yards farther out a second screen was built, also of poles and braced by wire. But the poles supported not canvas but wide-mesh wire-netting. The wire-netting reduced the speed of the wind sufficiently to diminish the pressure on the inner canvas screens.

Having been compelled to do classics at school, I could never have thought of anything so simple and effective. Nowadays a boy interested in the humanities has a choice of Sixth Form subjects. In our day it had been classics, without any option. Thank God that cruel tyranny has come to an end. Nowadays too I believe, every boy can get some basic knowledge of the Natural Sciences.

Standing one day at the outer screen and looking at the inner one, I thought the earth at one point on the outer side of the canvas screen looked worn, as if someone had been doing something. I looked closer. The edge of the canvas which was stretched over the balloon-bed, the canvas which formed the actual surface of the bed, did not look quite normal. It could be lifted. I lifted it. There, unmistakeably, was the end of a ladder. It was pulled out.

The ends showed it had been sawn through for convenience of transport or concealment. The Flight Sergeant was summoned. I said, 'Flight, this is half a ladder. Where's the other half?' I had to speak to the officers. It was not pleasant. They were all townspeople, as most men nowadays are. For them this countrywoman, this peasant, belonged to another world. They

Inflating a kite balloon with gas.

Repairing a kite balloon.

Two Artillery officers acting as observers fixing on their parachute harness.

could not understand that a good, sound ladder was of infinite value to her; it might be the most precious thing she possessed. Without it she could not pick her fruit, she could not stack her hay or anything else.

When I was but a very little boy, my father used to take me by the hand and lead me by footpaths about his first Derbyshire parish into the homes of his parishioners. Sometimes I went upstairs and saw those who were sick. I listened and looked. I learnt of men's cares and sorrows. I took it all in, while the grown-ups talked. Children miss nothing. They look into the eyes of grown-ups and read what they see, as do dogs. And they do not forget. In those days there were no buses, no cars. We were seven miles from the town. From the ages of 5 to 9 I went to the village school. I knew just how hard people were going to work when they left school, just how many worries their fathers had. The bigger farmers would be all right, but the little ones? Their life would be healthy, but hard. The big fellow, when he had got his harvest in, might go off to Bournemouth for a fortnight, but such men were rare. The little man with one cow or two could never think of such things.

I said that in my opinion there was only one solution. I could, of course, just report the facts to the representative of the French mission. He could then make his report. There would be a Court of Inquiry, endless delays, in the end probably the cost of a new ladder would be stopped out of the unit's pay. There would have to be a new ladder. A botched-up ladder would be no use to anyone. I proposed that the officers alone should bear the cost of the new ladder, each paying one quarter for, as I was now in Smith's place, I would pay his share. If they did not accept this solution, I should have to tell the whole story to the Colonel. They agreed.

Now I had to appear at the office of the French Mission. I suggested that if he would tell me what was the price of a new ladder, I would like to go and pay the woman myself. I should, of course, bring the receipt back to him. I felt that some personal act of penance, of retribution, was called for, and I had to admit too that I was glad to have an opportunity of visiting the little farm again. I like countryfolk and respect them. I feel it is an honour to be invited into a man's home, anywhere, at any time. I went, explained, handed over the cash. We had a good laugh and parted good friends. This good woman would not be telling her neighbours that the English were a lot of blackguards.

Why, you may ask, had I felt so bitter about this when, only recently, I had been a party to the projected stealing of a dog? But the dog was a living creature that could suffer, was suffering, and would be deformed. The farm, too, was quite a large one with a fine old house and good buildings. Robin Hood did not steal from the poor. A bad argument, that. But, you will object, the farmer would get another dog and he too would be deformed. I'm afraid we had not thought as far as that. We were only thinking about the dog in front of us. It must be admitted that I was so fond of Higman that I should have found it difficult to oppose any scheme of his.

No-one bore anyone the least illwill. I was, perhaps, childishly touched when a day or two later one of the officers, a Canadian of the Royal Highlanders of Canada, by name Fidler, addressed me as 'Skipper'. It was an acceptance of me as the head of the family, and there was an undertone of affection in the voice. Poor fellow, I was to lead him to his death.

Preparations were going forward for the great attack on the Messines ridge, under which was a gigantic mine which, on the appointed day, would kill in an instant a whole German regiment — the equivalent of a British brigade. Battery after battery arrived, new dumps sprang up, narrow-gauge railways were laid down. In the fields behind us a brand-new full-sized railway appeared, to feed these countless batteries with ammunition. Between us and the railway arose a huge R.E. dump. The guard was not so sharp on our side as towards the road, and the sight of stacks of duckboards made our mouths water.

Hydrogen was supplied to us in steel cylinders. These had to be manhandled from the road to the balloon bed, perhaps 150 yards. The manhandling of these heavy steel cylinders over wet slippery clay by men in gumboots was torment for them. Night after night, a few at a time, duckboards were abstracted from the R.E. dump until we had a proper track from road to balloon. This was an improvement. I had long since come to accept the doctrine that any government property which was not adequately guarded, was fair game.

Whatever else might come each morning there was always one envelope which I opened at once. It contained the target or targets for the day, together with the number of the battery that would do the shooting. This went straight into my pocket, and I showed it to no-one. If I ever found it necessary to pass a map reference to anyone I did so just before he left the ground. I made it a rule always to visit in the morning the O.C. of the battery, with which we should shoot in the afternoon, just to make quite sure that there was no hitch anywhere and also because personal contact does make a difference. It helps if the gunners know that the chap aloft is a man they saw this morning, and not just a number. Of course, too, I enormously enjoyed getting round seeing people, seeing what was going on.

How different this was from the small world of the infantryman! One morning I went to see a Canadian battery of heavy howitzers on the south side of the road running up to Plugstreet Wood. To my astonishment the gun-pits were empty. They must have pulled out during the night. In the ditch was a large roll of brand-new unused wire-netting. This was too good to be true, but it was true. As always, the Crossley tender had a spare man as well as the driver. Quickly we hoisted the roll up into the tender. Then I went off to visit an English field-battery. As we had a drink, I told them the Canadians had gone.

The young Battery-Commander said, 'Thanks for reminding me. They were going to leave me a roll of wire-netting. I'll send someone round to collect it.'

It was in my tender, a few yards away. I thought of our men slithering about on slippery duckboards, carrying heavy steel cylinders. This man had known the Canadians were going. He had had five or six hours of daylight in which he had done nothing. I kept my mouth shut. When we got home, very quickly the wire-netting was transferred to the duckboards.

Soon we were able to add another refinement. Someone spotted the fact that in the big R.E. dump, easily accessible at night from the fields, there were stacked sections of Decauville light-railway track, like large sizes of the track we used to run our little model steam engines on at home. By night a number of these were removed and laid from the road to the balloon-bed. There was no more carrying of heavy steel cylinders. It was only necessary to lift them from the lorry and place them across the rails and then, with a man at each end, they could be rolled along without effort.

Why was a supply of cylinders necessary? A captive balloon cannot have the open sleeve that a free spherical balloon has. It has a safety valve, carefully adjusted to open just before the balloon is quite fully distended. In warm, sunny weather the balloon may well lose some gas. So it must occasionally be topped up. It is the duty of the balloon guard at all times to watch the balloon on the bed and make sure that the pressure inside is greater than the pressure outside. There is always an ample supply of sandbags available, which can be hooked onto the rigging to pull the balloon down tight onto the bed and keep up the pressure. None the less, occasional topping-up is necessary.

After a balloon has been shot down and a new one brought up, there is a delightful gathering inside the new balloon before it is filled with gas. It is first inflated with air, thanks to a little Douglas horizontally-opposed twin-cylinder engine, such as used to be found in Douglas motor-cycles. The meeting inside, on the day I so vividly remember, consisted of the Colonel, Higman, myself, the Flight Sergeant and probably the chief rigger or the rigging corporal. The valve of a streamlined balloon, as this was, is not at the nose but at the side, at the point where the diameter is greatest. The valve line runs straight across and is made fast on the opposite side. There it is possible to make minor adjustments from outside. Once the balloon has been filled with gas, no-one can get inside to make any further major adjustment. This preliminary inflation with air is therefore of the greatest possible importance. In addition it makes it possible to inspect every part of the balloon carefully from end to end.

Why did I find this occasion delightful? To get in, each of us took off his tunic and boots, so that he presented a smooth surface everywhere, then lay down and wriggled in through the sleeve which had been disconnected from the blower. Inside we found ourselves moving noiselessly in our socks on the smooth fabric floor in a large hall, which had no windows, but which was full of a greenish light filtering through the fabric on all sides. This was indeed a fairy cave. Even the Colonel looked gnome-like, though I did not think it was wise to say so. However, we had not come together to meditate on the happiness of childhood's dreams. We had to get on with our job in a world full of the wickedness of grown-ups.

From the time I arrived at 32, the spring weather having arrived I was so busy that there was no time for visits to neighbours. But I managed to slip up to see my new neighbour Lee, Higman's successor at 25. He was a regular officer, a Captain in an Irish regiment, who had for a time been Military Attaché at Lisbon. Lee was an experienced soldier but he had not done the training course in England.

Proudly he took me round his domain and I found myself looking at my own old balloon with my former Flight Sergeant, the Liverpool policeman. Lee observed a hole on the under-surface. He said, 'What's that, Flight? You must get that patched.' The Flight looked at me: I looked at him. The hole was perfectly round. When air enters the scoop under the balloon, it fills the ballonet and the rudders. When all are filled, air is still forcing its way into the scoop. Some way of escape for the excess must be provided, and that was the purpose of the hole. If it were blocked, Heaven only knows what that result would be. I have no doubt the Flight's powers of diplomacy would have been capable of dealing with this situation.

Having taken over our sections on the same day, Lee and I proceeded to live in a state of most friendly rivalry. There was at all times keen rivalry between Wings and between the smaller units in the Wings. Lee and I had a little private rivalry of our own, which could lead to farcical results. One day I had finished whatever I had to do and was just sitting up there, enjoying the evening and keeping a watchful eye on everything in general. The light began to go, and there really was no point in staying up any longer. When I looked Northwards, Lee was still there, at about the same height. The light got feebler. It was really absurd. I rang up Lee and asked him what he was doing.

He said, 'Waiting for you to go down. I was wondering what you were doing. I can't see anything.'

I said, 'Well, that's just what I was doing.'

We checked our watches and agreed to start down at a given time. I gave the order to haul down and saw that Lee was beginning to move. It took about twenty minutes to come down 5000 feet. As I was watching the crew running to the handling guys, I happened to glance upward. Lee was stationary at least 2000 feet up.

I said, 'What the devil are you doing? You promised you'd come down when I did.'

He said, 'Oh no! I didn't. I said I'd start down at the same time as you. I did. But I said nothing about stopping on the way, and I've done so, just to have the pleasure of seeing you land a few minutes before I shall.'

One quiet afternoon it occurred to me that I might very well deal with administrative matters from the air. The elderly chap who ran the office and chart-room was in peacetime a traveller for the *Boys Own Paper*, which I had read long ago with great pleasure, especially when in the sick room. I asked him to read out to me whatever had come in.

There was a letter about fat. Fat was precious, and the Government had launched a scheme whereby units were to be encouraged to save fat and return it. The value of the returned fat would be credited to the unit, which would be able to draw extra rations to that value, rations of a relatively luxury type. Every unit was to detail an officer who would be responsible for the unit's fat. He would have to inspect it daily and classify it as first and second class fat. Not without a certain childish pleasure, from a height of nearly 5000 feet, slap bang in front of the enemy and looking straight at Messines, I dictated an answer to the letter about fat. When I went down, it would be ready for signature and time would have been saved.

That evening I put it to the officers, asking for a volunteer. Not surprisingly there was silence. I knew exactly nothing about fat. No doubt the others were conscious of the same gap in their knowledge. I had to say, 'As you know, I'm fully occupied all day. I just can't take on anything else. If no-one volunteers I shall have to detail someone.' It was Fidler, the Canadian, who said, 'I know nothing about fat, but if it'll help, I'll take it on.' So he became officer i/c fat.

One day I acquired temporary local fame. It was the old story of a hopeless day and someone keeping cave for the whole Wing. So there I was, alone in the sky. Very beautiful it was, too. There was a ceiling of cloud but the clouds were all moving down from the north, and'there was a dazzlingly bright shaft of light striking down through the clouds. Where it struck the earth there was a brilliantly illuminated almost circular patch. All around was dense shadow, purple and deep blue, rendered more intense by the contrast of the dazzling illumination of the patch. It was extraordinarily beautiful. I was watching this patch of light, as it moved southwards across Belgium towards me. It was so beautiful that no-one could possibly resist the fascination. Perhaps, too, as it approached, I might see something useful.

The illumination was so intense that for a moment one could see every detail of the area over which it was passing. Suddenly it struck Ypres. For a few moments I saw that legendary, tormented city. The ruins of the Cloth Hall stood out uncannily clearly, with a kind of ghostly beauty, dazzlingly white against the deep blue background. Then the light moved on, but the vision had bitten into my mind. Shells had been falling on Ypres. Shells were always falling on Ypres.

Suddenly there was a voice on the telephone, from the Wing, the Colonel himself.

'Is that you yourself, Hodges?'

'Yes, Sir.'

'What are you doing?'

'Enjoying the view, Sir.'

Later I heard from Higman that this reply had caused a
sensation and brought me fleeting fame. I was not being funny.
I gave a direct answer to a direct question. Apparently the
question had originated not from Wing, but from Army HQ.
How was I to know that? If I had known, I should have given
the same answer. But it is not the kind of answer that Army HQ
expects from people in the air. Fortunately it was well received.
I was regarded as a good chap.

One evening, when the Colonel had carried me off to the
Wing and we were sitting around the fire chatting, from the
background the Colonel said, 'Hodges, I believe you've become
a real balloonatic.' Coming from him that was the highest
possible praise. That night I went to bed feeling what I imagine
a man must feel like when he's got a VC.

My dearest friends had been killed. I had already begun to
feel that if anyone took an interest in me or I in him it was an
ill omen. The Wing ordered me to detail a despatch rider for
special duties. In addition to having heavy lorries, a mobile
telephone exchange, a mobile winch, we had Crossley tenders,
two motor-cycles with sidecars, two solo motor-cycles. I was to
part with one of my motor-cyclists. I picked the one I thought
the better of the two, though there was nothing wrong with
either of them. At first, maybe, he was not too pleased at the
prospect of leaving his friends, but he could not fail to realise
that he was really a lucky young man and that I had done him a
good turn. Instead of doing all kinds of errands in a more or less
forward area, he would from now onwards live at the Wing,
where he would be safer and probably more comfortable. Every
day we sent the report of the day's work to the Adjutant. If he
had time he would make a précis; if he had not, he would just
put the reports in a case, lock it, and hand it to the
despatch-rider.

The latter would then ride as fast as he possibly could to
Army HQ at Cassel. Having handed in his case and got a receipt,
the despatch-rider would then return to Mont Rouge, to Wing
HQ, and wait until the next evening. All he had to do was to

keep himself and his machine fit to blind like hell every day from Mont Rouge to Cassel, about twenty miles. This really was a soft job, and I felt I had done this decent chap a good turn.

Before long we heard he had been killed. Somewhere between Mont Rouge and Cassel a drunken infantryman had rolled across his path, and that was the end of him — but not of the infantryman. Now comes the strange sequel to this tale. After the war I studied at the Sorbonne. In 1920 and 1921 I returned to England for the summer vacation. My father's vicarage was three-quarters of a mile from the village of Barrow-on-Trent, which is a few miles from Repton. Our squire was a Burton brewer, James Eadie, an extremely kind neighbour. He would occasionally send a car to take my mother shopping in Derby. As our nearest buses were at least two miles away, this was a real kindness.

One day he had sent up an open car, not the big Rolls which took him to Repton station every morning and which we could always stop if we wanted a lift towards Burton. Mother was at the back with a friend. I was in front beside Marshall, the chauffeur. Him I had known already before the war. I gathered that during the war he had been driving a Rolls at Army HQ, but I did not know for which Army HQ.

Between Barrow and Swarkestone a motorbike overtook us. Marshall said, 'I don't like them things. Nasty, dangerous things.' I said, 'Oh! I don't know. I've had a lot of pleasure from mine.' He said, 'I hate 'em.' I said, 'You seem to speak with a lot of feeling. Have you some special reason?' 'As a matter of fact Sir, I have. I once saw a very nasty accident.'

Some hunch made me say: 'Was it during your war service?' 'Yes, it was.'

'Was it in the Second Army?' 'Yes.'

'Was it in the spring of 1917?' 'Yes.'

'Was it on the road between Mont Rouge and Cassel?' 'Yes.'

'Was it in the evening, about 7 o'clock?' 'Yes.'

'Was it an RFC despatch-rider?' 'Yes.'

'Did a drunken infantryman roll across his path?' 'Yes. Yes, he was accelerating out of the village down the long straight main road. The last house was an estaminet. Just as he came along, the door of the estaminet opened and this drunken infantryman came rolling down the steps and across the road. He couldn't miss him. Yards down the road he landed on his head. Broke his neck. Stone dead. I was first on the spot and picked him up. I hate motorbikes.'

It only remained for me to say, 'He was carrying my day's report.' So I had sent this decent young man to his death, and I had thought I was doing him a good turn. The infantryman was not hurt, just rolled over into the ditch. Yes, ladies and gentlemen, I can guess what some are thinking. I assure you I have invented nothing. It happened just like that. Marshall and I lived in the same Derbyshire village, and that conversation took place on the road between Barrow and Swarkestone where stands the great bridge across the valley of the Trent, the bridge which was held by the advance guard of the Highlanders, while the Pretender at Derby was deciding what to do next; the bridge which of old was the main crossing over the Trent on the way to London.

Coincidence seems to have played a large part in my life. I remember in the spring of 1915, the 1/4th Northamptons moved from Thetford to Norwich, spending a night at Attleborough on the way. As billeting officer I went on ahead to arrange billets for men and horses. My orders were that, until the battalion arrived, I was to billet myself in the Maid's Head. In those days the dining-room of the Maid's Head was the first room to the right of the entrance. This room, which contained a fireplace mentioned in the *Paston Letters*, was too small. I had to share a table with a correspondent of the *Morning Post*, who was in Norwich to report on the conference of the Independent Labour Party. He saw that I was wearing the badges of a regiment which was not stationed in the town, or perhaps I should say city, for Norwich is indeed a great and fair city. He knew I was not on leave, for he saw me speaking to a Sergeant after breakfast. He very much wanted to know what I was doing. I had no intention of telling him. We were not playing a game. We were engaged in a war for our country's existence. Every day at breakfast, lunch, dinner we had a little duel. He tried to trap me, to find out what I was going to do or had been doing. We got to Saturday morning. He was desperate.

I thought, 'What am I to do? If I tell him to go to hell, he'll get hold of one or two of my men, stand them drinks, get something out of somebody. I'm sorry, but for the King's sake I shall have to lie.' I told him we were looking for a car with a wireless set in it which had been guiding Zepps in towards London. He went off back to Fleet Street, quite happy. Some weeks earlier we had been doing just that, but the episode was over so I could safely make use of it.

At the table nearest the door sat a Staff Colonel, to whom, as I went past every day I said 'Good morning, Sir.' On this Saturday morning, the Fleet Street man had gone, the Colonel and I were the only people left in the room. I started to walk towards the door. To my no small alarm, the Colonel looked up from behind his *Times* and beckoned to me. As I approached, he leant over the table and said, 'Quite right, don't tell the bastard anything.'

In August of the same year, with one other officer and a hundred men, I had been for a week at A Beach, at Suvla, in Gallipoli, at the disposal of the Naval Beach Officer. I could not report back to the Regiment, because it had gone. The whole Brigade had moved away southwards, and was now on the left flank of the Anzac sector. We were left stranded.

Our orders were to report to the Commander of the Norfolk and Suffolk Brigade, whom I should find somewhere on the northern slope of the hills facing across the Gulf of Saros, towards Bulgaria. We crossed the hills. I chose a goat-track halfway up, and we followed it. The light began to fail. We saw Norfolk flashes and knew we were getting warm. It was now dark. I asked someone where I should find the Commander of the Norfolk and Suffolk Brigade. He said, 'Keep on along this track. You'll see him in a hole on the right.'

Leaving my fellow-officer with the men, I went on along the path. Presently I was looking down into a dug-out. There was a box, a candle on it, a Brigadier, four Colonels. What was I to do? Should I go in? Should I wait? I thought of my tired men. I stepped down into the hole and saluted.

The Brigade Commander did not say, 'Why this inter-
ruption?' He did not say, 'What do you want?' He said, 'My
friend, what can I do for you?' He saw before him a young
officer away from his regiment, away from his Brigade; with a
few words he had taken him under his wing, he had made him
feel at home. I said, 'Sir, I have to report to you with a hundred
men of the Northamptonshire Regiment.'

He said, 'Ah yes, I know. Just step back a minute, will you?'

Then he looked at me very hard and said, 'My friend, I know
your face. Now I wonder where I have seen you before.'

I said, 'Yes Sir, in the Maid's Head, at Norwich.' The
Commander of the Norfolk and Suffolk Brigade had been killed
or wounded, and my Maid's Head acquaintance had been
brought across from the Divisional Staff to take command for
the time being.

At 32 we had two motorbikes with sidecars. The driver of one
was so terrifying that he was reserved for parcels. One day I was
rung up from the HQ of No 2 Company at Nieppe. Major
Stringer, our old acquaintance of the First Army was there and
would like to come up and see me. All their transport was out.
Would I send something for him? It so happened that all our
transport was out too. Would a sidecar do? It would. I sent
someone across to the transport lines with a message that a
sidecar was to go to Nieppe. A few minutes later I realised with
horror that I had omitted to specify which sidecar. Of course
the wrong one had gone. Well, it was too late now. We should
just have to hope for the best. In course of time the driver
arrived, with empty sidecar. All I could get out of him was that
the Major had said he preferred walking. In course of time a hot
Major arrived, badly in need of a drink.

The road from Nieppe to us joined the main road from
Armentieres to Bailleul, which ran roughly east to west. A mile
or so from Armentieres the Neuve Eglise road came in from the
north at right angles. At this point houses or farm buildings
came right up to the corner, making the corner completely
blind. On one side was an estaminet. According to Stringer, the
driver came charging round this corner straight into the back of

a lorry standing outside the estaminet.

'Then,' said he, 'your blasted driver rose in his stirrups, let go of his handlebars and leaned forward with hands outstretched against the back of the lorry, crying at the same time, "It's all right Sir! It's all right Sir!" We ended up with most of the sidecar under the lorry and my nose half-an-inch off it. I got out and told him I'd finish on foot.' Written, that may not sound very amusing. It sounded very funny indeed as Stringer gave his account to the accompaniment of vivid gestures.

Our tenders were not allowed to exceed 20 mph. The idea, no doubt, was to economise on cars, tyres and petrol. I was so busy that for six weeks I had never had a chance to slip off to Bailleul for a bath. At last a dud day came. I had caught up with all the paperwork. Joyfully I slipped off to Bailleul. The baths were in the stabling of an old house. I was naked and in the act of stretching out a leg over the side of the bath, rejoicing in the steam rising from the lovely hot water, when a shaft of sunlight hit the wall above the bath.

I flung myself into my clothes, ran to the market place, said to Langstaff the driver, 'Forget all your usual orders. Drive back hell for leather. I take responsibility, and you've got a witness here in the spare man. Go on, drive like hell.'

As we were doing our best along the Armentieres road, another RFC Crossley overtook us. Back at the camp I shouted to the Flight to put the balloon up at once as I ran across for my parachute harness. In no time I was leaving the ground.

As I did so, a call came through from Higman. 'I understand you've been seen racing along the Armentieres road. What about it?'

I replied, 'I plead guilty. May I point out that we were overtaken by another RFC Crossley, going even faster. I didn't see who was sitting beside the driver, but I'm prepared to bet that the number on the back was the number of the tender you normally drive. May I also point out that when the sun came out, I was naked in Bailleul, but in spite of that I was easily first in the air. In fact, no-one else is off the ground yet.' I never got that bath.

There was a mounting tension in the air, as dumps and stores, light railways and guns, ever more guns accumulated. Yet there were still lighter moments. One afternoon one officer was up. Visibility was poor. Nothing was happening. Down below I was bored. From time to time I asked if he had anything to report. Probably I irritated him as Stringer had once irritated me. He was more tactful than I had been, and so could deal with the situation better. When I asked yet again if anything was happening, he said, 'If you think it will be of any interest, you may report that there seems to be considerable activity on the beach at Folkestone.'

There were even moments of pure farce. It was arranged that I should take up a New Zealand General and show him the country he was soon to advance over on the great day. He was the perfect John Bull, with a thick neck and a broad ruddy face. Higman would lunch with him at his HQ. I would lunch early, go up to see if conditions were favourable, and from the air would speak to Higman. If all was well, Higman would bring him round. Meanwhile I should be coming down to pick him up. A big shoot may take up to three hours. The general did not wish to give up a whole afternoon. So that afternoon there was no special target, but a New Zealand battery was standing by, in case anything turned up. As usual, during the morning I went round to see the battery.

On the way back we were passing the HQ of the New Zealand Artillery Brigade. I thought it might be a good idea to look in there and make sure there was no mistake about the date. As we stopped, the General himself appeared and, seeing us, said 'Ha! What a bit of luck! Lend me that car, will you?' We were mechanised, the gunners were not. This put me in an awkward position. I said, 'Well Sir, I've got to get home. If you don't mind coming round my way I can let you have the car after that. Will that do?' It would.

When I got out, Langstaff went off to Bailleul with the General; I went up after lunch. Conditions were perfect. I rang up Higman at the gunner mess. I told him we could go ahead and added, 'What the devil's going on down there? There's such a noise in the background I can hardly hear your voice.' He said, 'Can't tell you now. Tell you later.' The General arrived. He was put into a parachute harness.

I took the precaution of saying, in front of witnesses, 'You understand Sir, don't you, that when we're in the air I'm in command. If I say "Jump!", you jump at once without hesitation.' All went well for the General's entertainment. Unfortunately for them, I spotted a working-party working on a new light railway. The Germans too were making counter-preparations. We got the New Zealand battery onto them, one of the General's own. They were splendidly accurate. Chunks of line were removed. The first shots undoubtedly caught them by surprise. Only about a dozen shots had been fired, and the General had seen the country. Later in the day Higman came round and explained the cause of the mirth.

When Langstaff had taken the General to Bailleul they had parked in the market place. As the General got out of the car, he said to Langstaff, 'Get me some fresh lettuce.' When he had taken him back to his HQ, Langstaff had put into his hand a small, neat package. The General said, 'What the devil's this?' Langstaff said, 'You told me to get them for you Sir.' At lunch the General had told this story against himself. The resulting shout of laughter was what I had heard on the phone. I said to Langstaff, 'Why did you do that? Were you being funny?' He said, 'No Sir, I wasn't sure what he'd said. I looked at him and thought, "That must be what he wants".'

Perhaps inevitably someone asked, 'By the way, whose driver was it? Who'd trained him?'

Some gunners had a lonely life. There was an Australian field battery behind Ploegsteert Village, which lay south of the famous Plugstreet Wood. They had a forward command post right out in the fields, nowhere near anything. The chap out there wanted to shoot with us. As a rule we did not like observing for field-guns because the bursts really were not large enough for air observation. The 4.5 howitzer would just do. All the serious counter-bombardment work was done by 6-inch and 8-inch howitzers, sometimes by guns. I wanted to see this chap and talk to him. From the Neuve Eglise road two roads ran eastwards towards the lines; one disappeared into Plugstreet

Wood; the other, further south, ran up to Plugstreet Village, where it turned sharp right, parallel to the lines, and became what had been the village street. Either I could stop a long way back and walk up the fields — that would take a long time — or I could drive up to the village, which no-one ever approached, and then I should have to walk back only a field or two. This would save a great deal of time and time was precious. I said to Langstaff, 'No-one ever goes into Plugstreet Village, and I can't take the responsibility of ordering you to do so, but if you think you could drive me there I should be very grateful.' He said, 'Yes, of course, Sir.'

Off we went, straight forwards, and I did not look at the speedometer. As we came up to the village turn and slowed to take the corner, a Military Policeman appeared from under the earth and shouted, 'What the hell are you doing here? Get out!'

We did, but not by going back. We turned the corner and ran along the village street. This village had not been flattened, but it had been shelled and no house was intact. It was much too near the line to be healthy. Presently we came to a house, the front of which had been blown off. We drove into what had been someone's drawing-room. There the car would be invisible in case any German air patrol should pass over. I told Langstaff and the spare man that they were on no account to leave the shelter of the house, but were to wait there till I came back.

Then I crossed the road and wandered off down the fields. The Australian was delighted to see a visitor, for he was absolutely isolated and had had no visitor from the outside world for Heaven knows how long, if ever. He was not a little astonished to see someone approaching from the front, instead of by the normal route, from behind. When I got back to the village, the car was there but no men were to be seen. Here was a pretty kettle of fish. I knew of course that I ought not to have brought these lads so far forward. I felt sick with shame and anxiety. The fact that they had disobeyed orders and left this house did not help me in the least. I was the criminal. I should never have brought them to the place.

Here I was, cut off from everybody, with a car I could not drive, miles from home. To get me and possible corpses out,

Caquot kite balloon about to ascend. The basket is just leaving the ground. Air mechanics are holding the ropes and the motor-winch is seen beyond.

A Caquot kite balloon seen from the stern.

another car would have to be sent to this accursed place. Would the Military Policeman have a telephone in his dug-out? Yes, certainly he would. Sick with anxiety, as I have never been before or since, I went out at the back. No sign of life. I called Langstaff's name. No result. The gardens of the neighbouring houses were separated by walls. Parts of every wall had been knocked away by shells. I started to walk from garden to garden, called 'Langstaff, Langstaff', uncomfortably aware that there was only open country between these gardens and the enemy. I began to give up hope. They must have been caught by some stray shell.

At last I saw them, running towards me, their arms full of daffodils. The wretches! Little did they know what torments they had caused me. Never was a man more relieved than I was. I was too relieved to be angry. I realised suddenly how fond I had become of my scamps, who every day drove about with me from battery to battery. When I went to my room after lunch to get my parachute harness, it was full of daffodils, arranged in shell-cases.

In Gallipoli we had had the impression that the young Sapper officers, straight from Woolwich, marvellously trained, were in their early days a little bit too theoretical. They could produce a neat sketch, showing exactly how a position ought to be organised for defence. Then an old hand with local knowledge would point out a snag, which just spoilt the scheme. For instance, it might in theory be a good idea to deepen a trench which was not quite deep enough, and to use the soil removed to fill sandbags urgently needed for a barricade. If, however, the shallowness of the trench was due to the fact that a week or two earlier the Turks, the previous occupants, had thought fit to bury a few people under only a few inches of chalky soil, if an attempt was made to fill sandbags at such a spot the result would be that normally quite tough men would start vomiting. Of such little things is made the difference between theoretical war and real war.

One morning I visited an old Major who commanded a battery, a very seasoned old warrior. The dugout had a new concrete roof which was hollow — I think it was called a box roof. Just after me a young Sapper turned up, and began to talk most enthusiastically about this splendid invention, the hollow box of concrete. They were being produced in large numbers. Everybody would have one. There would be no more casualties as long as people were under their box roof. If a shell struck, the top layer would burst the shell; the lower layer, below the airspace, would stop the flying bits. From now onwards the Major and his officers would always be safe in their dug-out.

This very heavy concrete box was resting on clay. It seemed to me that if a shell landed not on the box but near the end, and removed a good large chunk of clay, the box would settle down and neatly flatten some or all of us. As I was only a guest, I felt it would be tactless to draw attention to anything so obvious. The old Major was getting more and more fed-up. The Sapper went on waffling about air-spaces. There was a dangerous look in the Major's eye.

Suddenly he said, 'Young man, I've been in these parts a damned sight longer than you have I can assure you; the only air-space here that is any use is at least a mile sideways.'

There was no time now for friendly visits. I was glad now that I had got about in the winter months and got to know people. On the rare occasions when I could let my mind wander, I used to feel proud to be in this line stretching across Belgium, continued to the south by the First and other Wings across France. Up in the north was Russell, then No 2 with Nelson and the great Gavin. Then came Lee, then me, and to the south of me someone I have not yet mentioned, perhaps the greatest balloonist of them all, Bolitho, known as Blot.

Why have I not mentioned him before? Perhaps because he is one of those people who are there, always calm, always reliable, devoted, fearless. An engineer I believe by profession, he was a lover of opera. He had a gramophone, one of the old ones, with a horn and a collection of operatic records. If the weather was bad or he had nothing to do, he shut himself up in a hut with his gramophone. Maybe that was what kept him so sane and calm. He had a safety-valve — I hadn't. I had noticed that all was not well with a lawyer from Jamaica. I had made myself speak to him, warn him, beg him to get a grip on himself. He did. Much later I heard he had been given command of a section and had done the job well for some time. In the end he had to be withdrawn to England.

Had the Colonel or Higman noticed anything odd about me, I wondered? I was always stone-deaf now for five minutes after I landed, although I had kept my mouth open all the way down. I was becoming impatient; I was astonished at the language I sometimes used. I was beginning to stammer and the stammer was getting worse.

It was a rule in the 2nd Wing that if we were attacked we should haul down, but we should stop at 1400 feet so as to be sure there was enough room to parachute safely. One day I had taken up the commander of a New Zealand battery, who had never been off the ground before. When we had just settled down at something below 5000 feet, a German fighter approached from the Lille direction. We hauled down.

At 1400 I said 'Stop!'.

The New Zealander, greatly agitated, said, 'Good God, man, what have you stopped for?'

I said, 'If we go any lower we shan't have room to parachute.'

The fighter changed his mind and sheered off. We went up again. I never got the New Zealander into the air again. Often I invited him, but he was not having any more. Once was enough.

On the days when I was dealing with New Zealanders or Canadians I found they just would not do business, however urgent, until whisky had been drunk. I had to acquire the bad habit of drinking whisky before lunch. Fortunately most of my work was done with English batteries. On one occasion when I visited a New Zealand battery for the first time, while I was speaking to the Battery Commander, he told a subaltern to pour out some whisky. I became aware of splashing noises inside a pint-sized enamelled mug, splashes which suggested the mug must be about half-full. It was. The Battery Commander came back with me.

Before lunch I showed him vertical photos taken by the plane people. He was tremendously interested and kept asking questions about places he knew as targets, or reference points, though he couldn't see them. Was that blob there White Farm? The damned blob seemed to me to be in movement on the photograph. After lunch we went up. I managed to see, but oh! what a headache I had! After that I was very wary and took a much firmer line with would-be too generous hosts.

It may have been noticed that I repeatedly speak of going up after lunch. We were lucky. The unfortunate Germans had to get up early and do all their serious observation with the morning sun behind them. We could get up and breakfast at a gentlemanly hour, pay visits and attend to administration in the morning and do our serious business in the air in the afternoon.

From time to time a balloon was shot down. On one dreadful day six were burning at the same time. It was a very neat operation. Two German pilots did the job, each one protected by two more, flying higher and behind. Assuming the balloons were numbered one to six, starting with No 1 in the north, one fighter shot up No 1, then wheeled south and dealt with 2 and 3. The other fighter dealt in the same way with 4, 5 and 6. The poor Colonel was in a state of frenzy, seeing his Wing in flames. This happened after I had gone, but I heard all about it.

7. Unforgettable Adventures

The old Drachen balloons were withdrawn and replaced by Caquot balloons, the invention of a Frenchman. Unlike the Drachen balloon, which had parallel sides, the Caquot balloon was streamlined, with three air-filled rudders. It was infinitely more stable than the old Drachen had been. To me it seemed as steady as a rock, but it was not necessarily so to people unused to the air. I once took up a gunner subaltern. He found it impossible to believe that I really had got my glasses on the target. After all, Naval people must have the same problem. No matter how violently the balloon might roll, jerk, soar, sink, kite — in some mysterious way feet and body adjusted themselves and the glasses were on the target.

He became so ill that I was really concerned for him. It was a rule never to interrupt a shoot, once it had begun The man looked so ill that I decided to take a risk. I said to the Battery Commander, 'Your man up here is so unwell, I'd like to take him down. Could you hang on Sir, for half-an-hour?' 'Nonsense,' said the Major, 'he must stay up there!'

And stay he did, though he could take no further interest in the proceedings. The Major was correct. If we had given the enemy a half-hour's pause, they might have used it to pull out, leaving us to shoot at empty gun-pits, or they might have got onto our guns, or both. An attack of any kind must be pressed home. I had not been wise. I had been misled by my genuine anxiety about this poor chap. Soldiering is a perfectly cold-blooded business — the heart must not be allowed to interfere.

On another occasion I realised this all too well. As the great day drew near, all leave was stopped. It was hard to have to explain to a man whose wife was about to have a child that he just could not have leave, that there was now no leave at all, none, for no matter what urgent, compassionate cause. There was no leave, none at all. The poor chap just could not grasp it. He went out looking ill and leaving me feeling miserable and hating life.

As the batteries massed, we sometimes found ourselves observing for a brand-new battery straight out from England. The first time this happened to me I was a bit uneasy. I soon realised how wrong I was. These fresh batteries were first-rate. They had been perfectly trained and were bursting to show what they could do.

In Gallipoli General Stopford had wrecked things at Suvla, partly because he did not really trust his Territorial troops. How mistaken he was! Well do I remember a night on which we were relieved on the hills between Suvla and the Gulf of Saros by a regiment of Irish regulars. It was, of course, desirable that the Turks should not be aware of this relief. Our own men moved noiselessly. The Irishmen were ill-disciplined and made such a devil of a noise that we could hear them long before they arrived.

A batch of us was withdrawn for a week and sent on a course to an Artillery School at Aire. There was nothing for us before breakfast. After breakfast we had an hour's lecture on some aspect of gunnery. Then we spent the rest of the day just watching gunteams handling different types of breech-block. The idea was that we should learn to understand the difficulties of gunners, and so not be impatient in the air. For a whole week we had no air-work, no responsibilities, no cares, no bangs, not even a distant sound of guns. There was nothing but the peace of a village. I was billeted on the village priest. In the evening he produced a bottle of wine and we enjoyed it by the fire. I did my best with my Higher Certificate French. He had been to Rome and showed me his photographs with pride. I retired early to a magnificently soft French feather-bed. Alas, all good things come to an end.

When the new Caquot balloons were issued, the first two in our Wing came to Blot and to me. When we rigged ours, we found there would have to be a change in the arrangement of the telephone cable, which was not indicated on the chart provided. In the Drachen balloon the telephone cable was taken straight from the basket to the head of the main cable, the point at which all the rigging, other than that of the basket, was gathered together.

On the new Caquot balloon this was not possible. The basket was slung in a different relationship to the main rigging and cable. If the telephone cable were rigged as usual, anyone using a parachute from the front of the basket would almost certainly foul it. The remedy was simple. We took the telephone cable up over the trapeze to a point higher up in the rigging, then down again to the head of the main cable. So there would be no danger. It seemed so obvious that it never occurred to any of us to send a warning word to Blot. If we had thought of it, it would have seemed an impertinence.

That afternoon a German fighter appeared suddenly. At first he appeared to be coming for me. Then he seemed to change his mind and swerved off towards Bolitho. I was ashamed to note that my first instinctive reaction was a feeling of relief. I soon had very different feelings. The German made straight for Blot. I could of course see everything clearly. The little flame appeared. Blot parachuted. His parachute opened and, caught by the wind, blew out horizontally across what must be the telephone cable. His riggers had not spotted the new difficulty and had fixed the telephone cable as usual. He was hanging on one side of it; the parachute was billowing out on the other.

Of the three possibilities, which would happen first? Would the balloon fall in flames, taking Blot with it? Would the telephone cable snap? Would, perhaps, some or all of the line from the parachute snap? The flame was beginning to spread. There was a pause which seemed endless.

Suddenly the telephone cable snapped and Blot was falling. He was swaying wildly, but the parachute lines had not been damaged or entangled by this strange misuse. Almost at the same moment the sheet of flame rushed along the length of the balloon. It fell so close to Blot that I felt the flame must catch the parachute. But it did not. Blot was safe. One of his tenders would already be racing after him.

Not many minutes later the voice in the chart-room said, 'Sir, someone wants to speak to you.' Peeved, I said, 'He can't. You know we never interrupt a shoot.' There was a pause — then, 'Please Sir, it's Mr Bolitho.' I asked the Battery Commander to stand by for a moment. Then:

'Is that you, Blot?'

'Yes.'

'Was it you I saw hanging from a telephone cable just now?'

'Yes.'

'Are you all right?'

'Yes, thank you.'

'What's the matter? Can I do anything for you?'

'I shan't have a balloon for the rest of the afternoon. I wondered if I might come up with you. It's such a wonderful chance for me to see Messines from your angle.'

'I can't come down now. I'm in the middle of a shoot. If you can wait, I'll come down when we've finished and bring you up. Come along, make yourself at home and have some tea.'

So it was done. Up he came to have a good look at Messines and proud I was to have him up there as a guest, for his was an almost legendary name. He said not a word about his recent experience; he might have spent the afternoon on the river in a punt.

As our guns massed, the Germans became more active. From time to time I was summoned to 3rd Corps, to the Counter-battery Staff Officer, a venerable and charming Colonel, who had a young lieutenant to help him. Well do I remember how one day he pointed to a map and said, 'The enemy have too many cannon hereabouts. We must do something about it.' Ever since, it has irritated me when people speak or write of cannons. I always told my own pupils that the plural of cannon is cannon, and that canons are elderly clergy. Why should everything be made dull and standardised?

There was one very good way of doing more damage. Those of us who had enough conceit or self-confidence sometimes took on two targets simultaneously with two batteries firing. It was really quite simple. For the afternoon one battery, no matter what its number really was, could be called A, the other B. When they were ready, each battery with its own target, you said, 'A, fire!' They fired. You observed the result and gave the correction. Leaving them to get on with it, you said, 'B fire!'

They fired, you observed and gave them their correction. Meanwhile A were now ready, so you said, 'A, fire!' and so on. This was quite an exciting game which called for complete concentration. It could be tiring. Only once did I stay up for more than three hours of real work and I never asked anyone to stay up for more than three hours. I once stayed up for five hours, to make sure that an important job was really finished.

We did not keep our glasses fixed on the target; this would be unnecessarily tiring for the eyes. Before the shoot began we got the time of flight from the gunners. If it were 55 seconds, having noted the time when the gun was fired, you waited until 50 seconds had passed, then you put your glasses on the target. At first you began by looking at the target continuously, but as you gained in experience and confidence, you gradually reduced the margin to 10, then 5 seconds.

The Germans, well aware that a great deal of movement must be going on at night, started a campaign of so-called night-strafing. Every night cross-roads, road-junctions, even rest camps were shelled. In a rest camp close to us the Australians had casualties. Every night the enemy guns searched about the back areas — it began to get on people's nerves. There seems to have arisen a legend that British commanders were fools, and that there was a feeling of distrust or disloyalty between officers and men. Nothing could be further from the truth. Our army was a happy one. I never saw our Army Commander, Plumer, but I always thought of him with respect and affection. There was a general feeling abroad that nothing foolish would be done, no unwise risks would be taken, there would be no unnecessary loss of lives. However, just at this moment there was a kind of irritation. People were saying, 'Why isn't something done about it? Why do we lie down under this?' In fact there was going to be a most effective reply — of that I will tell presently.

The Germans lengthened out to their extreme range. One shell fell short of the balloon bed, but a bit of shell-case punctured the balloon. It was repaired at once, but this was too much of a nuisance. I asked for permission to move balloon-bed and camp out of range. Our winch worked on a road which ran diagonally to the front. The Colonel disliked extremely anything which looked like a withdrawal; he thought it was bad for morale and my own instincts worked the same way. I pointed out that the winch would still be using the same road: so far as our work was concerned, there would be no withdrawal. I wanted only to shift the camp from the front end of the road to the back, so that the men could live and sleep in safety and the riggers would not have to turn out in the night and clamber about on a rolling balloon, looking for punctures to mend by the light of electric torches. He agreed. It could not be done in one day, but we began. A new balloon-bed had to be made; then the huts went one by one. There came a night when there remained on one side of the field the hut for the guard and on the other, right in the corner, my hut and the mess hut. The Flight-Sergeant stayed with the guard and, if anything happened, he would be responsible for clearing that side. My servant was in the mess, next door to me. Whichever of us woke first would dash out and wake the other.

Weary, I went to bed. Sometime later there was a mighty crash which rocked the hut. I shot out of bed, grabbed leather flying-coat and slippers, dashed to the mess to make sure that all was well with the other chap. Then I made off, having to cross a wide dyke with water at the bottom. This was quite a respectable jump. I made it but, as I landed, one slipper came off. The Germans had certainly got our old camp taped now. More shells were falling on it. We had moved only just in time.

Now I had to walk across wet plough-land with a bare foot. I looked at the wet clay. Mighty crashes were coming from across the dyke. They were much too near. I looked at the wet clay. I thought, 'No damn fear! I'd rather die here,' and set to work to look for the slipper. The Flight-Sergeant appeared saying, 'I heard you across the field, Sir. I thought there must be something the matter.'

There was a tremendous crash, a huge flash. A gentle little voice said, '*No bon, Monsieur.*' On the far side of the dyke, in the corner of the camp, standing out clearly for a moment in the great light of the shell-burst was a slender girl-mother, her babe in her arms. We managed somehow or other to get babe and mother across the dyke. With a charmingly dignified '*merci, Messieurs*', she made off across the dark fields towards Steenwerke. No hysterics, perfect calmness, perfect manners. There was no need to say more than '*Merci!*'. The way she said it was enough.

When I am asked why I am so fond of France, the first picture that comes to my mind is that of this young mother illumined by the flash of the shell behind her. True, we were in Belgium, but only a few fields from France. Then I think of an old saddlemaker in Bayeux. As I got off the bus from Arromanches, in the days before it had been made famous by the D-Day landings, there was a snap. A vital part of the sling of my artificial limb had snapped. By good luck I found an old saddler only a few yards away. Being in France, I removed trousers and leg in his shop, and he did his work, using first-class materials. He was stone-deaf.

I wrote, '*Combien?*'. He said, '*Vous êtes blessé de guerre, Monsieur?*' I wrote, '*Oui.*' He thought, then said, '*Deux francs, Monsieur.*' He did not want to charge anything at all, but he was too polite to do that. So he charged this absurdly small sum.

I was once in Chinon with three Bedford VIth formers, walking up the hill towards what is left of the chateau in which Joan of Arc met the Dauphin. We were travelling light, with little luggage. I had no other trousers than the pair I was wearing. I found the seam had split and I was becoming indecent. I said to the boys, 'You'll have to go on alone to pay your respects to Joan and the Dauphin. I must find a tailor.' There was one quite close by. I explained, and removed my trousers. He brought an armchair and the day's paper. When he had finished, we had quite a long conversation about the state of Europe. He refused any payment, saying he considered the conversation was payment enough.

I came out of the church of St Ouen in Rouen with a little niece and found she was in tears — the button had come off her shoe. Walking along, we found no shoe shop but an invisible-mending establishment. I went in and explained. The whole personnel stopped working, gathered round my little niece and comforted her, while a button was found and sewn on. Payment? What an absurd idea! It was a pleasure to do a little service for a child.

In Rouen too a garage-proprietor refused to put a new tyre on one wheel, saying that the tyre in use was good for another week at least. He was thinking of my pocket, not his. True, he was not being asked to supply the tyre which I had brought with me from England; but he had lost the job of fitting it because he was a conscientious man.

In the little town of Barr, in Alsace, I went into a garage and asked Madame if someone could put '*de la graisse dans ma cheville*' (grease in my ankle). Madame said, '*Pardon Monsieur, je ne crois pas avoir bien compris.*' I repeated the request and struck my leg to make things plain. Madame opened a door, uttered a cry, everyone gathered around while the job was done. Was I a '*blessé de guerre?*' Yes I was. That settled that. From that moment onwards life was embarrassing. In the hotel, if I appeared on the stairs carrying the smallest package, people rushed forward to take it from me.

In 1928 when there was a British Legion pilgrimage to the battlefields, I was a billeting officer in Amiens. I visited every house in a working-class quarter of the town. Everyone was kind and helpful. One old lady took me upstairs to show me a room in which floor and furniture shone from much polishing. With a dignity worthy of Versailles at its best she said, '*Je regrette, Monsieur, je n'ai pas de pot. Mais on fait ce qu'on peut. Voilà un sceau.*' (I'm sorry, Sir, I have no jerry. But one does the best one can. There's a bucket.')

My slipper was found; we made our way across the fields to the new camp. My admirable servant was standing under a tree, with all my uniform and underclothes over his arm. I ought to have mentioned earlier that one of the disadvantages of a captive balloon is that it acts as a lightning-conductor for the whole neighbourhood. Static electricity could be troublesome. One day the headphone was suddenly lifted off my head and fell over the side. I pulled it back and at once said, 'Haul down'. I was not waiting for any more.

The nearest AA battery to each balloon unit reserved one gun for the defence of the balloon. By an odd chance we found out what their technique was. When the balloon went up, they trained the gun on the basket and just followed its movements. When an attack came, they could just switch the gun left or right as required. One day a German attacked. The officer on the gun was a new man, just out from England. He had never fired a gun in anger. He was so excited at the sight of the real enemy that he forgot to switch the gun.

The poor devil in the basket was suddenly aware of a mighty explosion and bits of shell were whizzing through the basket, past his nose and his seat. None of them hit him. He parachuted at once, without waiting for more, and who could blame him? Fortunately his parachute had not been damaged. It may be that he was in such a hurry that he forgot that possibility.

A secret order was issued. Army HQ were going to deal effectively with this terrible strafing of the back areas. By this time there were guns wheel to wheel across Belgium, or so it seemed, and in places there was more than one line. On the appointed day every gun in the Second Army would fire from 9 to 9.5 pm rapid fire, each of course with its own target. If there was any reply, this would be repeated from 11 to 11.5 pm. This applied to every battery, from the heaviest down to the field-guns. I was to go up and watch the result. I was given no special instructions; any normal observation would be impossible. Presumably Army would want a kind of running commentary, a general impression. The only thing not filled in was the date, for which the code word was Smith.

Days passed; a week; a fortnight perhaps. It was all very

hush-hush, and I had not said a word, not even to my own officers. I was in the air every day and busy on the ground, engrossed in day to day activities. One morning Higman rang up quite early and said, 'Your new equipment officer Smith is coming tonight.' I said, 'Someone's made a mistake. We have no equipment officer in the unit.' Higman: 'Oh yes, you know, a chap's coming to you. I told you.' Me: 'Impossible. We have no equipment officer. Something's gone wrong.' Higman: 'You're crackers. I'll come and see you later on.'

I wandered around, wondering what on earth had gone wrong. Had Higman suddenly gone crackers? Had he been overworking? What on earth could this mean? About two hours later it suddenly dawned on me. I dashed to the nearest telephone and said to Higman, 'It's OK about the equipment officer. I'm sending a car for him tonight.'

All that day I was in a state of excitement. I should not tell the Flight to put up the balloon until 8.30, if then, but I must make sure that he and everyone else would be ready. I need not say why. Even when the balloon went up, I need not say what was the object.

Somewhere about 7 o'clock Higman rang up. There was thunder about. Unless I got further orders I was not to go up. Too often in life do such things happen. And yet, and yet, bitter as these moments are, every now and then there comes out of the blue some quite unforeseen happiness. My luck was out this time. Something was going to happen, which the world had never seen before and would probably never see again. I had been deputed to go up and watch. Now I could not.

As the time approached I advised people not to turn in, saying that at 9 o'clock there would be something worth seeing. It was a beautiful night in May. Everything was still. If anything was going on up in the trenches, we could not hear it. There was no sound on either side; the Germans had not yet begun their nightly misbehaviour.

This is where I fail. I just cannot describe what happened — could anyone? Barbusse perhaps. Most people, nowadays, have heard the boom of a field-gun coming from a television set. It is quite a respectable little bang. Imagine that several thousand guns fire at the same moment, a mass of guns the width of Belgium, covering the whole front of the Second Army. They all fire at the same moment. At one moment there is the gentle stillness of an early summer night. Then there is a roar the width of Belgium. And they do not fire once. They go on firing as fast as they can. And they are not all field guns. A lot of them are big fellows — 6-inch and 8-inch howitzers. The mighty roar goes on and on. Where there was darkness, there is a sheet of stabbling, savage flame, a sheet of flame the width of Belgium.

We all stand silent, overwhelmed by this flaming din. At 9.5 the roar stops dead, like a hellish but well-conducted orchestra.

Here and there a German battery replies. I tell people that there will be a repeat performance at 11. Some go to bed; many come out again and stand about as before. At 11 the same overwhelming roar; at 11.5 the orchestra stops. The silence seems even stranger than it had done at 9.5. This time there is no reply. No one says anything. We go to bed.

How comforting that roar had been to the hearts of all who were sick of being shelled in back areas! How beautiful that great sheet of flame had been! I have heard preachers who assumed that beauty, truth and goodness are necessarily linked together. Divine attributes they may be, but can there not be beauty without goodness? A mighty bombardment certainly has beauty, if seen from the right end. But goodness?

The Germans learnt their lesson. There was no more back-area strafing. From now onwards people moved by night unharassed and men in rest-camps slept in peace.

Some weeks earlier — it must have been in April — Higman and I had a strange experience together. He had decided to spend the afternoon in the air with me. The target was a battery which had been a great nuisance to the neighbourhood for some time past. Why it had taken so long to find it I cannot remember, if indeed I ever knew. There were various methods employed. There was sound-ranging. The plane people produced detailed photographs. We heard talk of agents behind the line. When down in France on the farm we had been warned to be on our guard against the latter. If we had anything important to discuss, we went for a walk up the orchard. In the farm itself shop was taboo. Probably they were quite harmless, though I had found before we left that, although they had professed to understand no English and I had to use my Higher Certificate French, the boy — either at school or in contact with troops — had learnt enough English to understand ordinary conversation.

Somehow or other this troublesome battery had been located. When the gunners were standing by — in fact they must already have fired a ranging shot — a voice from Wing said, 'Blizzard approaching from the north. All aircraft to land immediately.'

'Blast,' said Higman, 'this damned battery may pull out and we shall have all the trouble of finding it again. Meantime it may do a hell of a lot of damage. Oh, hell! It's your balloon. You're in command up here. I can't order you to stay up. Anyhow, you've just had a direct order to go down. That settles it. Hell! What a bloody shame!'

I said, 'Higman, do you seriously consider it's worth risking the lives of two officers to make sure of getting this battery?' He said, 'Yes.' That made my mind up. I said, 'Very well, we'll stay up here.'

I don't think he was expecting this answer. He had not been bluffing: he was not a fool. But perhaps his bitter disappointment had for the moment caused him to lose control of his tongue. Now there was going to be no going back. I would not have let him change his mind if he had wanted to, and he did not want to. He was enjoying the situation and, in all honesty, I was too. The Wing spoke: 'No 32 Balloon, repeat previous order, land immediately.'

I ignored that. Everyone else was well on the way down. The sky was emptying. From the north a great black mass was bearing down on us. After a pause the Wing spoke again: 'No 32 balloon. For the third time repeat order, land immediately. Take no further responsibility.' We stayed put.

It arrived. Once again I must admit there are things I cannot describe. The noise, the din, the uproar were unbelievable. Since that day I have had some idea of what the noise must have been

A line of three kite balloons probably an apron.

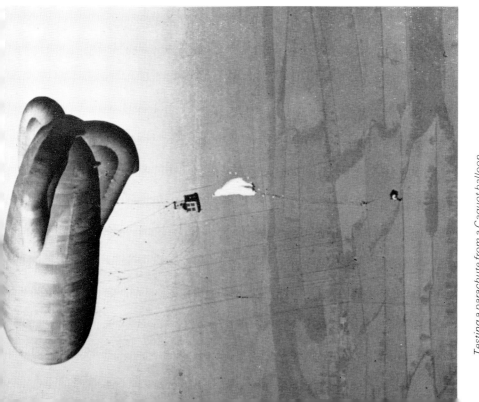

Testing a parachute from a Caquot balloon.

A British kite balloon falling in flames. Near Boyelles, February 1918.

Balloon apron as used for the defence of London.

at times on the old sailing ships in high winds. The wind was howling and whining through all the lines of the rigging, as if all the devils had been let out of hell and were really enjoying themselves. The big handling guys were flying out horizontally, as if they were just bits of string.

The dense mass of flakes was moving seemingly horizontally. It was wonderful to see them streaming past, not only overhead and on either side of the basket, but underneath as well, wonderful to look down into this white flowing mass, to feel that the storm was not passing overhead, but that one was inside it, right in the heart of it, entirely cut off from the world below. Wonderful! Splendid! But oh! how cold it was.

We cowered down in the basket, knee to knee, our eyes glued on the wind-speed indicator and on the barometer. The danger was the gusts. A steady wind would not have been so alarming. It was the gusts that produced the violent changes of strain. The wind would rise from 30 to 40 to 60, then fall back again, then up to 60 again, then back again. We were waiting for the moment when the windspeed would drop to zero. That would mean that we had broken away. At the same moment the needle of the barometer would whirl round and go off the dial, because the balloon, when it parted company with 5000 feet of steel cable, would shoot up into the heavens like a rocket.

That would be the dangerous moment. There would be such an extreme expansion of gas that our lives would depend on the setting of the safety-valve. If it were a shade too fine to cope with such abnormal conditions, the balloon would burst. Even if this did not happen, rising at such extreme speed, it would have so much upward momentum that it would overshoot the level which corresponded to the amount of gas remaining. Not having enough gas for this height, it would start falling and, if we were not wide awake, would gather a dangerous downward momentum.

We should have to watch for this moment and start putting out ballast at once to check the rate of fall. We should have to nurse her down very carefully, not having an enormous amount of ballast, and hope for the best. If the worst came to the worst, we could parachute and abandon the balloon, but that would be an act of despair which would not be regarded favourably.

The wind meanwhile would have carried us at great speed and at a great height far away down into France. The wind would be blowing in a straight line, the trench line down below was far from straight. On which side of it should we land?

Such were my meditations, in so far as it was possible to think at all in such a hellish noise. It had once happened that a balloon broke away, taking a lot of cable with it and flew slowly down the line. It was a new Caquot balloon. The Germans fired at it because it was an enemy balloon. The British fired at it because they did not want a specimen of a new type of balloon to fall into enemy hands. The result was a very uncomfortable trip, but neither Germans nor British hit it.

We cowered down with our eyes glued on the dials. It seemed as if this wild shrieking, this beautifully flowing stream of white coldness would never stop. The mass seemed less dense. There was more space between the flakes: the wind lost its speed: the din diminished. I began to see out between the flakes. I said to the gunners, 'Stand by! We're still here!' As the last flakes passed I said, 'Fire!' The Germans must have had the shock of their lives.

Nothing was said the next day. After all I might well have been arrested that very afternoon. No doubt the Colonel had had words with Higman, and, he being the kind of man he was would have taken all the blame upon himself. The battery was destroyed.

One day I was attacked. We had plenty of time to see him coming and I had hauled down, but before I had got down to 1400 feet he was on top of me. He had disappeared from sight. There is a large area of sky which cannot be seen by reason of the big streamline balloon overhead. When the balloon is up, there are two machine-guns down below with an officer in charge. He said, 'He's just diving on you.' I did not jump. I had felt very frightened indeed once or twice on the ground in Gallipoli. In the early days in Belgium I had occasionally wondered what on earth had made me leave my regiment. A burning balloon is rather an alarming sight. But in the air I did not feel scared. I felt interested, excited, enthralled, but frightened — definitely not. The Almighty just happened to have made me like that.

Usually people jumped as soon as the attacker fired. Mine had not fired yet. I have never understood why he did not fire as he dived. He dived on past the balloon, having for some time of course been invisible to me. Then he came in sight, came round in a great bank and swept along on a level not with the balloon but with me in the basket. For a fraction of a second I saw his face quite clearly at the other end of his gun. Why did he not fire? Why didn't I jump when I saw him coming back? In the first place, I was really intrigued by what the man was doing. When he had the great big gas-bag just below him, why hadn't he fired into it? Why, when he turned and came back, did he ignore the balloon which he could have raked from end to end? Instead he flew level with me, quite literally looked at me, then made off home at high speed.

I felt no enmity for this man, but a kind of sympathetic, almost friendly interest in what he was doing. In the second place, there was something strangely fascinating about the situation. As he attacked and dived, the AA gun and the two machine-guns were firing away merrily and there was quite a lot of noise. When he turned and came back, he wisely so manoeuvred so that they could not fire at him without hitting the balloon. After all the noise it now seemed very quiet. There was no sound other than that of his engine. I was quite conscious of the fact that hundreds of eyes down below were watching, waiting for the coup-de-grace, like spectators at a bull-fight. I was on the edge, ready to drop.

People down below must have thought I was crackers. I had really left it too late. But I might still drop and hope for the best. But I didn't.

There was a third reason. There was in me a mighty obstinacy, the same feeling I had had when the blizzard was approaching. Though I do not think I should have had the guts to stay up on that occasion and do my Nelson act if Higman had not prodded me; like him I was angered by the thought that anyone or anything should get between me and my target. We had defied the blizzard and destroyed the battery. This man had come between me and my work. He meant me to leave this balloon. But it was not burning yet and I damned well would not leave it until I was forced to. I have no doubt that more than once in my life obstinacy has made me foolish.

Certainly, on that day, as we looked at one another, I just felt 'Be damned to you!' Alone up there, we were having a little private battle of will-power.

He had gone. To the winch I said, 'Let up.' To the officer on the ground, 'What's the matter? Are there some of our fighters about?' 'No,' he said, 'the sky's quite empty. His gun must have jammed.' I always assumed that that must be the explanation.

Years later, in the middle of the Second War, I told this story to the Commander of a Fighter Squadron. He said, 'Hasn't it occurred to you that there might be another explanation?' Astonished, I asked what that could be. He said, 'It would never occur to any normal man that a fellow could be such a B.F. as to stand in a basket and gaze at him. He probably thought you were a dummy, full of High Explosive. That's why he beetled off for home. You probably pulled off a really first-class bluff!' It is a pleasant thought.

Later again, after the Second War, a friend who had served in the Balkans in our First War, told me that at one point enemy fighters repeatedly crept up behind a ridge and shot down a balloon. Tired of these repeated burnings, the balloon people got permission to put up a balloon with an explosive dummy in place of the normal observer. The enemy fighter made its usual approach and fired. There was a mighty explosion and the attacking plane fell to pieces. This would no doubt result in the circulation of a warning to the Luftwaffe, and my opposite number may well have thought that the strange creature in the basket was an explosive dummy.

8. The Work Continues

The whole question of courage and fear is very mysterious, at least to most of us. Judging from my own experience, when the moment is reached at which there appears to be no hope of avoiding death a man feels quite calm. On Hill 60, the Gallipoli one, I used to tease my friend Guy, fellow Kingsman, because he so very much disliked being shelled. Heaven knows, I disliked it too but not so much as being sniped. Shells are very unpleasant, but there is nothing personal about them. They are not aimed at individuals. Bullets are. On three occasions I have known that bullets were being aimed at me personally. The first time I was very scared and finally amused, because the situation was so ridiculous. The second time I was scared to death. The third time I was surprised and irritated.

Brought up in a Christian home, the L-shaped garden of which wrapped itself round the churchyard, from earliest childhood I had learned to look on death as something quite natural. Thinking about it in Gallipoli at a time when I was not sure how much faith I had left, at a time too when I saw little if any prospect of getting off the place alive, I still felt there was nothing to worry about so long as one was thinking quite selfishly and not thinking, for instance, of parents. If there is a future life, what a glorious adventure it would be to go out and see what it is like. If there is no future life, it doesn't matter a damn anyway. In any case, why worry? On the other hand, I do not at all like pain. I didn't at all relish the possibility of being wounded, especially of being blinded.

At Suvla I was on duty for a week at A Beach. On the last day I was able to slip away for a bathe. When I came out of the water, blood was pouring from my right hand. There was a deep cut across the fleshy part at the base of the thumb. Swimming in shallow water, I had struck the bayonet of a man who had been killed and was lying in the water. With my left hand and teeth I applied by field-dressing. The next day I rejoined the battalion and went back to my platoon. It was isolated, on the right flank of the battalion, from which it was separated by a gulley with steeply sloping sides and a perfectly flat sandy bottom. On the other side was a gap of some hundred yards between us and the next British troops. There was nothing to prevent Turks infiltrating at night and relieving the very troublesome sniper, who commanded the neighbourhood from a rounded hill which closed the gulley at one end.

In the heat of the day, when I thought he might be asleep, I had a good look at this hill. Later in the afternoon I was sitting in the dug-out, which had been captured from the Turks, when a voice said, 'Do you want anyone shot around here?' The voice came from an Australian sergeant. He was a super-sniper, a hunter of snipers. I said, 'Yes, I'll show you whereabouts he must be.'

I came up the four steps until I was half out of the ground. He was squatting on his heels. Our heads were close together. I was pointing to the curve of the hill. Suddenly there was a *pht!* between our heads. I shot back down the hole and he came after me. Unfortunately I was not quick enough in withdrawing my left hand from the second step; his heel came down on it and he turned on it. It was rather a mess. He tied it up, and now I had two bandaged hands. The next morning the hands did not look too good. The soil of the Turkish dug-out was not particularly clean and some of it had been ground into my left hand. I decided I would rather be shot than die of blood-poisoning. I should have to cross that gully. If there was still a sniper on that hill, he could not help seeing me.

As I was certain to be hit, there was no need to make a fuss about it or indulge in any dramatic stunts. I walked down the steep path to the flat floor, walked across quite slowly without any hurry, went up a long smooth sloping surface of rock and into the next gully where were the Battalion HQ and the MO. He soon had me nicely tied up again. I started back with two brilliantly white new bandages.

Early in the morning there had been a slight shower of rain, the only one I remember during my five weeks on the peninsula. As I started to walk down the rock slope, my feet slipped and I went wallop, flat on my back. At that precise moment there was a *pht!* across my stomach. I leapt up and ran like blazes. I got a clear start of about 20 yards, perhaps a little more. The man must have thought his shot had brought me down. Probably he had laid his rifle down and picked up a pair of glasses. For the last 80 yards or so he was firing at me. The silly man should have aimed at some fixed point ahead and waited till I got there. He had lost his head and was taking pot shots at me. Each bullet seemed just to miss the small of my back.

It's extraordinary how fast you can run when you've really got to. Though you are already going flat out, the sound of a bullet makes you accelerate just a little bit more. I felt such an ass doing the part of the running target, that it made me laugh to myself.

I think everyone who has been through a war will agree that when there is really no more hope you cease to worry. I was sure there was not really a hope and felt amused. I might be asked, 'Why not stop and stand still?' That would be un-sporting. The man who is playing the part of the running target must play the part out to the end. I dashed up the track and flopped into the trench. My platoon, of course, had seen all this, but they could not do anything to help me.

Later on, though Battalion HQ were still in the same place, our Company was on the left, on the hills running up to the Gulf of Saros. By daylight we were isolated, except for the field telephone. To reach the battalion we had to cross the rocky slope with a little scrub on it, up over a skyline, slap bang in front of Turkish machine-gunners a few hundred yards away. Obviously any movement across that slope and skyline by daylight was out of the question. Rations and mail came up by night. One day a man was shot through the stomach. We had to keep him with us lying in the shade of a bush till after dark.

Early on the morning of August 21st my Company Commander sent for me and said, 'You're wanted at Battalion HQ at once. Go off now, before the mist rises. I've no idea what it's for.' Off I went in the white morning mist, and I didn't tarry. The Adjutant was John Brown, later the famous Sir John Brown.

He said, 'The Brigade say a message must be taken personally by an officer. The message is: "The attack will begin at 2 pm" ' (or it may have been 2.30, I can't remember). We had our own private regimental code words. I said, 'Surely this message could have been sent in code.' He said, 'Yes, I thought of that, but they are afraid it might be intercepted and the code broken. They say secrecy is so essential, it must be carried by word of mouth. Nothing else will do.'

I pointed out that my chances of arriving were practically nil, and I hoped he had already begun picking my successor to make the second attempt, and perhaps a few more after that. He shook hands with me solemnly, as with a man about to go to the guillotine. I asked if the message must be taken immediately. He said, 'No — any time up to midday will do.' I walked slowly up the gully. Meeting the Regimental Sergeant-Major, I had a chat with him, making it last as long as possible. Then I came across the MO and spun out the conversation as long as possible. I explained what I was doing or about to do, and he played his part with understanding. No one else seemed to be about. I couldn't just sit down and meditate on death.

I went on up the gully, till I found the Machine Gun Officer right at the top, peering very cautiously with glasses through a thick bush. He was very worried when I told him I was going over the skyline . . . I've sometimes thought the poor chap must have given me his last reserve of nervous strength, for shortly afterwards his nerves went wrong. In the end he was killed. He was Crockett, a member of one of the great Northampton boot families.

For a time I sat there, and he peered through the bush. Very soon though I felt, 'Hell! I can't stand this. If I've got to be killed, let's get it over!' I got up, turned round, jumped up over the skyline and started running madly down the slope. The machine-guns started up at once. Bullets were spattering on the rocks. I was zigzagging like mad. The slope was steep and each stride was more like a leap. It was something like the style of the Guides' Race at Grasmere Sports. I just zig-zagged like hell, and then suddenly I was on my tummy safe behind the line of stones which served as a front line on this rocky ground, which was too hard for digging. I was safe.

Having got my breath and pinched myself to make sure I was still there, I could crawl along to the Company Commander at the other end. This took place on August 21st 1915, the day of the great attack across the Salt Lake, the last great attack of that campaign.

My third Gallipoli scare happened when I was bathing, north of Anzac. When a sniper's bullets strike the water quite close to you, you feel most horribly naked.

The reader may well ask — 'Why this digression?' The answer, I think, is that balloonists are human beings who have hearts and memories. Human lives are not cut up into convenient sections such as those beloved by historians. All my Gallipoli memories were then very fresh and, as I went about my business I was thinking, remembering, making comparisons. On the Gallipoli occasions I had been very scared indeed. In the air, facing this chap with his gun, I had not been scared.

Somewhere away behind Messines there were still some batteries which had not been satisfactorily located, and they were doing too much damage. It was decided to try an experiment. I looked straight over Messines. To the south, the right as we looked at it, the line of the salient drew back sharply round Messines. From his position south of me Blot had an oblique view of my area. If we both went up at night and both balloons were plugged in to one chart-room, when a German gun fired we should both get a bearing on the flash. When our lines were plotted on the map, the point of intersection of the two lines would give the position of the battery.

We always observed through graticuled glasses. We should need the equivalent of graticules on the ground. As we should be working in the dark, these reference points would have to be lights, so placed that the enemy could not see them though we, of course, could. In those days there was no electric lighting on cars. Carbide was the source of light for head and side lamps. We should want one headlamp in the middle and two sidelamps to mark the flanks. Was there a road which would serve our purpose? Fortunately there was, and I already knew it. It was the side-road which Whitfeld and I had taken to visit the gunners on the day of the famous long walk in the winter, the walk which ended with our sitting on a manure-heap. Plotting on the map showed that lamps judiciously placed would exactly serve our purpose.

There was a first visit to have a good look, do some careful pacing and mark the three spots. The low ridge which masked the battery from the enemy would also mask these lights. There would have to be a second visit to drive in some more substantial stakes. The lamp party would have to find the exact shot in the dark.

The second trip turned out to be amusing. This side-road left the road at right-angles not many yards before it dived into Plugstreet Wood. Though the Germans had done most of their back-area strafing by night, they now paid attention to a few roads by daylight. This road-junction was one of their chosen targets. Approaching at a little after 9 am we saw shells falling on it. Perhaps 200 yards short of it there was quite a gathering behind the buildings of a farm still more or less intact.

The Germans shelled this road-junction every morning. They started punctually at 9 and stopped equally punctually at 9.30.

What was the result? After the first or possibly second morning there was never anyone there. Those who wanted to pass that corner queued up behind the farm. With them was a fatigue party, and there was a supply of brick-ends and other suitable material with which to fill up holes. At 9.30 the last shell fell, the crowd came out from behind the farm, the fatigue-party filled the holes, lorries could move forward, life went on again. This daily farce was continued for about a fortnight, if my memory serves me right. Blot must have been making similar arrangements. Where he had put his lamps I had no idea; that was his business, not mine.

When the night came, Higman came up with me. Both balloons were plugged in to my chart-room. It was a beautiful night, but there was ground mist below us. The Germans were very nervous. Could they perhaps see us, looking up through the mist? Was the mist in fact not so thick as it appeared to be when seen from our height? Further away on higher ground there was little, if any mist. Perhaps they had received a warning from people behind them that we were in the air. Or was it just an attack of nerves, such as does befall people in trenches from time to time? They were behaving as if they expected an attack or a large-scale raid. Flare after flare came up through the mist and broke, now white, now coloured. Very lovely it was, this free firework show seen against the pure white of the mist from which it rose.

For a long time nothing happened. Farther back behind the lines, all was still. I was very tired. Higman suggested we should sleep in turn. I went to sleep. The basket of a big free balloon is comparatively roomy; the basket of a captive balloon is narrow. When you sit on the canvas seat — when observing you normally stand — your elbows are out over the sides. If there are two up, your knees are touching. It was delicious to go to sleep in this clean air, high above the earthy fug down below, but the sensation of awaking was extraordinary. I suddenly found myself apparently just sitting in space, not yet sufficiently awake to realise that there was a large balloon just overhead. The panic down below seemed to have died down. Only occasionally did a big white flare light things up for a moment. We sat there enjoying the beauty of the night. The people in the chart-room must have been bored stiff. At long last, far away, a German heavy fired several times. We had him fixed, for we could see our lights perfectly. How bored the men must be out there with the lights. The German gun had obligingly fired several times. Our night's work had not been wasted. The position would go to Corps and possibly to Army. That battery would soon be destroyed.

We came down: Higman went off; the balloon was put to bed. Everyone turned in — everyone except me. I sat down to await the return of the lights party. It didn't return. After half-an-hour I began to be uneasy. Had something untoward happened? The stray shell? I told the guard to wake a side-car driver. He appeared. I got in. With dismay I realised I had once again forgotten to name the driver. I had got the chap who was reserved for parcels. Our side-road, on which the winch worked, ran into the road which ran south from Neuve Eglise. We turned to the right, southwards. We should have to take the next turn to the left, up the road to Plugstreet Wood. I said, 'You know the way, don't you? Next turn to the left.' He said, 'Yes, Sir!' The poor devil had been dragged out of bed and was probably still half-asleep. Presently I was rudely shaken by a series of mighty bumps. He had turned up the new railway and we were careering over the sleepers. I got out and helped to lug the bike back onto the road. It was a P & M, as were all RFC motorcycles. They and the Crossley tenders were remarkably robust. They never gave us any trouble, no matter how brutally they were used over the most impossible surfaces.

We found the turn we should have taken and found a truly impressive movement of traffic in both directions, or rather lack of movement. The road, which in the hours of daylight was rarely used by anyone, was a main supply route at night for all the units ahead. With the enormous massing of guns, the night traffic of those bringing up rations and ammunition to all these new units was added to the normal night life. New batteries were still arriving. Weary with long travel, they were in strange country and had, presumably, to be conducted to their new positions or else just find them by map reference. There would be delays. Traffic was flowing back. But forward movement was made difficult by batteries which had halted. Edging our way with most feeble lights between the traffic line and these motionless batteries, we passed several batteries with normal teams. There was one battery of what must have been much heavier guns, drawn by splendid great draught horses. How pathetic and ghostly they looked, sleeping as they stood, heads lowered, utterly weary, their drivers asleep on their backs.

I had known extreme weariness in Gallipoli, but never before had I seen anything of the exhaustion of noble animals. How long had these splendid, patient creatures been on the road? Mercifully the Germans were making no attempt to strafe this road. It is fair to assume that they had been demoralised, at least for a time, by the mighty bombardment of that memorable night on which every gun in Belgium had fired. For one great mercy man may be truly thankful. Mechanisation has taken horses away from the beastliness and suffering of war.

At long last we saw our tender coming towards us. I got out and ran across. Very basely I said to the Flight-Sergeant, 'Change places with me, Flight, I want to talk to Mr Yorkshire.' It was true, I did want to talk to Mr Yorkshire. But the Flight knew quite well that I wanted to get out of that sidecar and I saw dismay in his eye. When at last I thought I could turn in, it was found that a young sergeant was missing. No-one seemed to have any explanation. That was the end of hope of sleep for me. All through the night and the next morning I was inquiring, searching.

Toward the end of the afternoon I was called to the telephone. The Colonel was speaking. 'Hodges, I hear you're still looking for this sergeant. You must get some rest.'

'Sir, is that advice you're giving me or is it an order?'

'It's an order. We want you in the air. I shall ring up again in two hours' time and, if you are not in bed then, I shall have you placed under arrest.'

From the crossroads at Messines a road ran southwards with a hedge on the side nearest to us. In this hedge were the gun-pits of a battery which had been very troublesome and was much disliked in the neighbourhood. The Counter-Battery people at Corps HQ had decided that it must be destroyed. For this job 250 rounds of 8-inch were allotted. It was not easy to see just where the guns were. Fortunately we had fine vertical photos, taken by the plane people. One was an old one, taken when snow was on the ground. If a gun is fired over snow, it stains the snow. Before firing a gun over snow, wise men lay sheets on the snow in front of the gun, assuming of course that they have sheets to lay. It is not easy to place the sheet in position, or to remove it when the firing is finished, without marking the snow. Some careful sweeping may have to be done. A powerful lens may reveal variations in the surface of the snow.

We started with the left-hand gun-pit. When we had had ten direct hits, we moved on to the second, then the third, finally the fourth. When we had had ten direct hits on each gun-pit, we had got through 70 shells. What should we do with the remaining 180? It seemed to me very likely, almost certain, that they would have local dumps of ammunition near the guns. There was no hedge on the far side of the lane. The country was open and I could see no sign of any work having been done anywhere. We had better search the hedge. We started at the north end, worked down to the south, back to the north, down to the south again, and so on all the afternoon. I did not miss out the gun-pits we had already hit. They took their luck. We went up and down, up and down.

When at last we had finished, I had been in the air for five hours. The gunners must have been as fed-up as I was. Our patience had been rewarded. From time to time there was an impressive explosion. Whenever we got through to ammunition, there came up tree-like columns of smoke of strange, weird beauty.

I went down, sent Yorkshire up for the rest of the evening and sat down to a welcome cup of tea. Higman turned up and we sat side by side, drinking tea. Like everyone else, he was pleased that this battery had been blotted out. I had noticed, as I got out of the basket, how pleased the balloon-crew were. Suddenly there was an almighty crash. We dashed out across the field, down the road to the winch — that crash could mean only one thing. The balloon was being shelled. Up to now we had always been attacked by fighter aircraft. This direct attack by gun-fire was something new. The winch was just beyond the range of their guns and the balloon about 5000 feet higher, even more so. They had removed 9-inch guns from naval vessels they were no longer using and had manufactured shrapnel for them. Normal 3-inch shrapnel is not pleasant; this 9-inch shrapnel was the very devil, for it covered such a wide area. They had selected Nos 2 and 32 for the experiment.

Of course I did not know about No 2 until later. I was concerned only with trying to save my own balloon. The balloon was not at its full height, the road we were on ran diagonally to the front. I let up and set the winch in movement towards the rear. We were altering the range in length, height, direction. The Germans were in no hurry and had a plane overhead spotting. After the third round I saw the nose of the balloon was becoming concave — they had hit it.

Did Yorkshire up there know this? Now was the moment for him to parachute, while there was still some gas in the balloon. I could not tell him so because the telephone cable had been cut. Perhaps he'd been hit. We would have to get him down. How? The balloon would soon be empty. We should have to fly it empty, as a kite. To make that possible there would have to be a tremendous pull on the cable, a very quick descent.

I said to the winchman, 'You are going to be given an order which you've never been given before. You may think it sounds crackers. Never mind. Do exactly what I tell you to do, and do it immediately. Now, put the winch into top gear.'

The winch had two gears. The top one was used only when there was little wind and the throttle was opened very little.

'Open up the throttle gradually until it's flat out.' The tremendous pull on the cable flew the balloon very nicely as a kite. When the handling guys were approaching the ground and rigging approaching the winch, I said 'Stop.' Yorkshire had long since realised what was going on. When the winch stopped and the balloon began to fall, a hand shot out on either side of the basket, each hand holding a thirty-pound sandbag which was dropped. Yorkshire then jumped up and hung by his hands from the trapeze. The basket, with the remainder of the ballast and the instruments, took the first bump. Yorkshire was none the worse for his experiences, though he was certainly ready for a whisky or two.

While the balloon was being flown as a kite there were other things going on down below. When the Germans, doubtless informed by their plane, knew they had hit the balloon, they turned their attention to the winch. When their accursed 9-inch shrapnel came down in our direction I realise that Higman and I were the only people in the neighbourhood with no tin hats on our heads. We had dashed out just as we were. I said to the nearest airman, 'Run back into the lines and bring the first two tin hats you see. Be as quick as you can.'

In no time he was back. I took one and put it on my head; Higman did likewise. In spite of the fact that we were engaged in a critical operation, I just became helpless with laughter. Tin hats do not suit all faces. Higman had a fine face with features of the type commonly described as Roman. The tin hat on the top of this face looked irresistibly comic. The owner of the hat had been using it as a candlestick and the top of it was covered with candle-grease. Projecting proudly from the top was the candle. I roared with laughter. Higman, obviously thinking I was going crackers, was very angry. He then looked even funnier and I laughed still more. At last I managed to say, 'Look at your helmet.'

A shell burst unpleasantly low, just above the winch. An airman, with the natural ostrich instinct to put something between himself and the next one, leapt forward and crouched in front of the winch. It was moving, certainly very slowly, but it was moving and it weighed eight tons. The driver of the winch lorry could not see him. I opened my mouth to yell a warning. Higman was quicker. He was also better placed. He was in line with the crouching airman, who was facing the other side of the road. He took two quick steps forward and gave the man a tremendous kick up the behind, which sent him flying across the road into the ditch, thereby possibly saving his life.

Later in the evening we heard about No 2. That too had been hit and Gavin had parachuted. The lead from the parachute ended in a spring hook, of the type used on dogleads although, of course, very much larger. The lead from the parachute harness ended in a metal ring which snapped into the spring-hook. There must have been a flaw in Gavin's hook. His friends, watching as he came lower, saw that his hook had opened. It had opened so much that the ring was now on the extreme tip of the open hook. If the hook opened any more, the ring would drop off. It is easy to imagine the anxiety of the watchers during the last few hundred feet of the fall. Fortunately Gavin himself did not know what had happened. If he had known, he might have reached upward or made some movement, and that would have been the end of Gavin.

The failure of the hook was reported to RFC HQ. Next morning orders were issued cancelling the type of parachute connection hitherto used. We were to make a new type, with materials that were available on the spot. A loop, with a runner which would draw it tight, would be slipped over a boxwood toggle.

A new balloon was brought up during the night and the next day we got down to the usual routine of inspection and rigging. I had everybody working on the balloon. I was so desperately keen to get it up as soon as possible, I thought one rigger could finish one parachute while I had lunch, then he could work on the other two while I was up in the afternoon. When the Colonel appeared he was very pleased; we had got on much better than had No 2. There was no doubt that we should have a balloon up again after lunch. He asked about the parachute. I explained that all the riggers were working on the balloon and that as soon as he had gone one would start on one parachute, which I should use that afternoon. The other two could be done while I was up.

He was extremely vexed and disappointed. There was great rivalry between the Wings. He had hoped to be able to report that the changeover was complete in his Wing. He could not do so. His agitation made him stammer more than usual. He cursed me soundly.

When he paused, I said, 'Excuse my saying so, Sir, but what you've just said proves this order reached me at least two hours late.'

He said, 'Yes, Hodg-Hodg-Hodg-Hodges, I qu-qu-qu-quite agree with you. There is a bl-bl-bl-bloody fool at the other end of the line, but you must admit there's one here too.'

I was standing beside the road, with what I thought was a perfectly blank expression, waiting to give him a farewell salute. The strain of recent nights and days had been severe – I was very tired. I was conscious of the fact that the Colonel's eyes were fixed on me. Suddenly he jumped out of the car, smote me hard on the back and said, 'Cheer up Hodges. All the same in a hundred years.' Before I could pull myself together and give him a decent salute, he was gone.

For another reason that day was memorable. Higman had rung up. I realised at once that he was not his normal self. There was something unusual in his voice. He said, 'That shoot you did yesterday afternoon — you reported that the battery was definitely out of action. Are you sure?'

Me: 'Of course I'm sure. I shouldn't report direct hits if I hadn't seen them.' 'I knew you'd say that. Well, the trouble is that the morning plane patrol has reported that the battery is in action. There's hell's own row going on behind the scenes. The plane fanatics are saying this proves that balloons are no use and are just a waste of money. Much better to spend the money on more aircraft. I knew you'd stand by what you'd said. I said I trusted my man, that it was his word against another man's, that in fairness I must insist that they send out their best man on a special patrol. Meanwhile you'll do exactly the same shoot again this afternoon, and I'm to come up with you to watch you do it. I'm sorry. Those are the orders I've been given.'

So this looked like the end. What a humiliation! I saw myself being sent back to my regiment. I crawled around, feeling utterly miserable. Life had been so good. What had gone wrong? I had seen all those direct hits — the battery could not be in action. What did it all mean?

Late in the morning I was called to the telephone. It was Higman, and it was the usual, happy voice — in fact it was jubilant. The patrol had gone out, photographs had been taken: every gun had been destroyed. What had made the morning patrol think it was in action? During the night the Germans had moved up a mobile AA gun and turned it down horizontal. When the morning patrol was over them they fired and produced a nice big flash. When the patrol came back, they had moved to the next gun position and fired from there. Then they withdrew the gun and looked forward to watching us using up another 250 rounds, destroying a battery which had already been destroyed . . . I wonder, were they far-seeing enough to hope they might also damage the reputation of balloons, which were doing so much damage?

Somehow or other the Counter-Battery people had found out, or had been informed that the main reserve of ammunition for this battery was under the farm just north of the Messines cross-roads. It was to be destroyed, and again there was an allowance of 250 pounds of 8-inch. It was a fine farm, of the normal local type. I could see clearly the front of the house on the far side of the court or enclosed yard. House and buildings seemed to be more or less intact. I did not like this job of destroying a farm. There was no clue as to where this dump was. 'Under the farm' can mean many things. It might not necessarily be under the buildings. Where was the approach? If the entrance was not in the buildings, it must be very skilfully camouflaged. I could see no sign of it. Should we search about, as we had searched the hedge? A large store would probably be deep, possibly with a lot of concrete above it. To penetrate that we should have to hammer at one spot. But what if we chose the wrong spot and merely made a deep hole, while the dump remained untouched, perhaps really quite near? In such a case a miss is as good as a mile. I had been left a perfectly free hand. If anything went wrong, it would be my funeral. This was going to be a colossal gamble. I would choose one spot and stick to it. But which spot?

The house was of the usual one-storey type, with the front door in the middle. If we were going to have a look at that farm, what should we do? We should enter the yard by the double doors, now closed; we should make our way round the yard, the middle of which was occupied by the manure-heap, to the front door and we should knock on the door.

We would knock on the door. I cannot remember where the first shot went to. The second landed plumb on the doorstep, and as it was 8-inch there was not much house left. I did not like this moment, the dissolution of a good farm house. We stuck to it — always I brought them back to the same spot. The non-gunner may ask, 'If they've been put onto a target, why can't they just be left there? Why must the observer continue to observe?' A shell travels through many layers of air at various heights. At any point in the trajectory there may be in the air a change of temperature, of wind-speed or direction, and guns get hot. We stuck to it. Fifty up and no result, but we were getting deeper and deeper. Suppose we got to a hundred and still nothing had happened? Should I call it off and try making another hole? But where? We went on. At 70 it came. Yes, I remember the number. When we had finished destroying the guns we had used up 70 rounds, and I remember thinking, 'Here is yet another strange coincidence. With the 70th round we've got through to the ammunition.'

What a sight! That too I can still see. There rose a great pillar of dense, yellowish smoke, not spreading, going up and up, perhaps 80, perhaps 100 feet or more; then it spread out at the top, like a weird tree. It was the shape with which we have been made so familiar by the photographs of atomic bomb-explosions, though of course very much smaller. It was impressive. We had produced this fantastic explosion. We had got there. I hoped it would rejoice the hearts of the men in the line.

Of how we used up the remaining 180 shells I have no recollection at all. My memory seems to snap at that point, as I look at that huge explosion and feel the enormous, wonderful relief of tension. Yet I think it must have been on that same day, or was it perhaps the next, that something strange occurred. After a bigger job, I think the one I have just described, I had to attend to what appeared to be a minor target, an anti-tank gun, cunningly sited. It commanded a slope up a shallow valley, an easy approach, which would certainly be used on the Day, and the very fact that for the first time we were asked to attend to one relatively small gun showed that the Day must now be very near. As usual I let it have a number of direct hits, probably my usual 10 – I cannot remember. When I wrote the report I stated how many direct hits had been obtained. Then a strange feeling inside me, a feeling of horror, in fact of fear, made me sign without any final summing-up.

I think it must have been the next morning that a call came from the Counter Battery Office, 9th Corps. The voice said, 'I have here your yesterday's report of the shoot on the anti-tank gun. You report repeated direct hits, but you have not said the gun is out of action. Would you mind telling me why?'

I said, 'Sir, I was an infantryman for two years. I realised what an awful slaughter there will be if that gun is in action when the infantry go forward. Something made me hesitate at the last moment. I'm sorry, Sir, it was stupid.'

A very kind voice said, 'I quite understand. Now would you please, tell me, just as man to man, what do you really think? Is that gun out of action or isn't it?'

I said, 'Sir, it is out of action.' I knew it was. Why then had I been so stupid? Was my nerve going? Was I just a bit too tired? As I had had my glasses on that spot, I had seemed to see in that shallow valley slaughtered infantrymen, a gun firing into infantrymen. On the Day did the Germans manage to slip another gun into that place? Was there a slaughter? There is second-sight in my family. I have known several clear cases. Was my fear justified or was I just overtired and seeing things? I had an unpleasant feeling that my nerve had begun to go. There was no hope of leave or rest. The Day was coming.

9. No More Shooting

An order came out inviting applications for Regular Commissions. Evidently they were looking ahead now, preparing for the postwar period. There were to be special courses at Sandhurst. I had been happy with my regiment. I was happy with these good people in this Wing. I enjoyed my contacts with the Corps, the sight of the great maps in the Counter-Battery room. I had seen things from an angle so different from that of the regimental officer. With our Wing covering the whole of Belgium, with the daily view of great stretches of country, I had begun to realise how interesting Staff work could be.

Here was something to satisfy a man's ambitions, the battle of wits, the pitching of mind against mind. Already in Gallipoli I had realised I should never be able to come home and be a priest, as my father and grandfather had been. Already in the autumn of 1914, as I brought a tired platoon back into the village of Beyton, near Bury St Edmunds, I had shouted, 'Come on, pull yourselves together, look as if you had bought the whole damned village,' not knowing that the Adjutant was in the offing.

A minute later, as I made for the mess, he joined me and said, 'If you get through this show you'll never go back to civil life. You'll stay in the army.'

I said, 'Oh no! I'm going to take Orders.'

'I bet you £5 you don't.'

One morning in 1916 at a point opposite Suez, I was talking in the Company Office to the Company Sergeant-Major. He had a little son aged, I think, 12. Foolishly I said, 'I suppose Sergeant-Major, you've no idea yet what he's likely to do when he grows up.' With a pained voice he said, 'Oh Sir, as soon as he's old enough I shall put him in the regiment.' He was really shocked by the idea that any officer could possibly have asked such a foolish question. Some, I suppose, would find this funny. I did not. Rightly or wrongly, I have always thought that loyalty is something to be admired, even when misdirected.

I should have to take this order across and make it known to the other officers. If I was to put it to them as a good idea, and it seemed I ought to do so, they might think or even say that it was up to me to set a good example. Very well, I would. I asked Higman to find out what the Colonel thought about it. The Colonel thought it was a good idea, and I applied for a form on which to apply.

An order from the Wing. I was to reconnoitre a route by which to advance when the Day came. The balloon would have to be manhandled across country. We should have to choose and mark a route which avoided roads, so as not to get in other people's way, to find the easiest spot to cross every dyke, to avoid lines of trees and even perhaps specially big isolated trees, to take care to miss any lines laid by Signals. Fidler, the Canadian, was a very neat worker with a mapping-pen. I asked him to come with me. We turned northwards, towards Neuve Eglise, to get clear of the Plugstreet Road, stopped the car short of Neuve Eglise and took to the fields. Presently we were in a lovely meadow. The sun threw the shadows of the trees across the grass. It was a heavenly May morning. Here was no noise of war. Frogs were croaking round a pond. To the north the jagged outlines of what was left of Neuve Eglise stood up not far away.

In this bright sunlight with the fresh green of the trees about them, they looked not at all suggestive of war, death, suffering. They looked like some romantic folly in a park or even a stage-setting. This did not seem to be the real Neuve Eglise we knew. It was etherealised. The frogs croaked, the pond sparkled.

We were in no hurry to move on, to begin the real work. We sat on a bank and pored over the map, comparing it with the ground ahead, deliberately prolonging our sojourn in this little haven of peace. In the end we had to go ahead. We had a nice peaceful walk in the fields, always choosing the best way round or over every obstacle, and Fidler plotted it all on the map. This too happy outing had used up most of the morning.

However, when we got back to the camp I thought, if we wasted no time, there would just be time to go and see the Commander of the battery, for which I should be observing that afternoon. This was especially desirable for I did not know them; we had never worked together before. Moreover we had an unusual target. We were to blow away the trenches on the curve of the salient in front of Messines, not a pleasant job. The mere fact that we were now turning our attention from such targets as batteries and dumps to the very line itself showed that the Day must now be very close upon us.

I collected a map and some photos and got back into the car. It would have to be a very quick trip and a quick lunch after it. Just as we were on the point of moving off, Fidler appeared round the corner of a hut. I hailed him, 'Hi! Fidler! You'd better come with me. You don't know these people I'm going to see. You'll be sure to be observing for them before long. It's a chance for you to get to know them. Come on!'

We had had a happy morning together. This would make a nice finish to it. We took the road that would, if followed long enough, lead to Plugstreet village. The battery was short of this, on the left or north side of this road, which ran on eastwards to the deserted village. I felt it would be unwise to leave Langstaff on the road with the car. I told him to take the car back to the last farm we had passed, an empty one with buildings only slightly, if at all, damaged, to turn off the road and put the car out of sight behind the buildings and wait for us there. We would walk back to him.

As we left the road and walked northwards across the field, a meadow, the heavy howitzers were in a hedge on our right, from which, if my memory is correct, rose a row of poplars. Facing us, on the left flank of the battery and a little to its rear, was the little farm house in which was the battery HQ. It had a thatched roof and lilacs all around it, all in blossom, a charming picture. For years to come I was to hate the sight of lilacs. In time I got over it — I planted lilacs in my own garden and gave some to a friend. Yet even now, when I see the loveliness of a lilac, my heart goes back to that May morning in Belgium.

The door was in the middle of the long side of the house. We turned right and so came into the battery HQ, installed in what was normally the kitchen. Immediately to the left of the door was the map-table, set up in front of what at other times would be the kitchen stove. The Battery Commander stood facing his maps and the wall. His subaltern, a very tall fellow, was looking over his shoulder. At the corner of the table stood Fidler. I was on his left, between him and the open door. In the background were a telephonist and a clerk. There was also a South African NCO who had arrived almost at the same moment as ourselves to talk about ammunition supply. As our business was more urgent than his, he was waiting in the background.

I was leaning across the table, holding out before the Battery Commander a fine photograph of the trenches we were going to blow away, the trenches on the curve of the Messines salient.

The photograph had gone. So had the Battery Commander. I could see nothing, hear nothing. I could feel nothing under my feet.

I thought, 'Well, I suppose I must be dead.' I had felt as though something had hit me very hard on the back of the head. Possibly my head had struck a glancing blow against the doorpost. I seemed to be floating in space. Then I realised I was not dead, and it gave me no pleasure at all. None. I felt like a boy who has been made a monitor but who has been demonned. When I thought I had moved on, here I was back again. Moreover beams, chimneys, God knows what broken things were falling, and falling on me. Instinctively I put my hands up behind my head to try to protect my head, for I had turned over in the air and was now face downwards.

When things stopped falling I could hear terrible groans. I found that if I kept quite flat and, stretching my arms forwards, dug my fingertips into the cracks between the bricks, I could pull myself forwards. The violent explosion had squashed me like a concertina. I was gasping, but taking in not air but fumes. I must get to the door, get some air into my lungs and then go and help those who were groaning. I stood up and fell against the wall. Puzzled, I stood up again. Again I fell against the wall. A third time I stood up, and again I fell against the wall. I looked down. Now I understood. I could see the insides of my left foot.

The ankle had gone and part of the leg. My first thought was, 'I shall never walk over the fells again.' The foot was waving about on the end of a kind of string. It was no longer a question of helping others. If no one helped me, and quickly, I might not live much longer. I hopped to the door, out of it, then along the side of the farm, with the instinctive feeling that I must get what was left of the farm between me and the next one. The hopping hurt. I looked down again. There was a hole through my right leg, but the bone was not damaged, nor was the artery. I went on hopping.

As I turned the corner, when I got to the end of the house, I found myself face to face with the farmer. I must have been a nasty sight. Though I did not yet realise it, blood was spattered over my tunic and cap. The farmer, poor devil, had just seen a great part of his house blown away. I wanted to put my arm round his shoulder to steady myself and get some of the weight off my one foot. He looked at me with eyes full of horror and panic, and ran.

It was normal practice if a battery was obviously going to be shot up and was not actually in action, to remove the breech-blocks and clear out. Looking around, I saw on the far side of the field behind the farm a khaki back disappearing into a wood. I collected all the strength I had got left and let out a yell. Rather to my surprise, the owner of the back heard it, realised there was something wrong, turned round and came running forwards towards me as fast as he had a moment before been running back in the search for safety.

He was a New Zealander, a lieutenant. He was wearing, not the New Zealand hat, but an ordinary service cap. I was wearing my Northampton tunic, for seconded officers were allowed to wear the uniform of their regiment.

He got me onto his back. In those days I weighed nine stone. He started off at right-angles to the line of fire, in the hope of getting out of the danger area. By a most extraordinary fluke the first ranging shot from a 9.45 had landed plumb on the battery HQ. When we had covered about 200 yards he stopped and we sat down on the edge of a dyke, the line of which he was following. I gave him my parachute knife. We always carried a good sharp sheath-knife, with which to cut ourselves free from the parachute if we were in danger of being dragged. He took my left leg across his knee, the idea being that he should cut away this useless foot.

At that moment the second ranging shot arrived. It was nowhere near the target. It passed over us, fell in the field behind us and bespattered us with bits of field. I said, 'For God's sake let's get out of this bloody place!'

He handed the knife back to me, got me on his back again and off we went once more. I think he must have carried me about three-quarters of a mile. My one and only thought was that I must remain conscious, so as to help him by holding on. He was wearing a beautifully cut brand-new pair of riding-breeches. These were now drenched with blood.

He said, 'I say, old man, you've absolutely ruined my bags.'

We came to a small farm, and our luck was in. A New Zealand Field Ambulance was just leaving it for their new battle position. They stopped their last vehicle and got a chest off it. I was stretched out on the kitchen table and my leg was bandaged up. By this time I was feeling, to put it mildly, pretty mouldy. I asked my New Zealander to write his name and regiment on a piece of paper and slip it into my tunic pocket. I dictated two signals, one to the Colonel, the other to one of the surviving officers of 32 Section, to tell him to take over.

From somewhere they produced a very old Ford ambulance. I was alive enough to be amused by this ancient vehicle, for only recently in some paper or othef I had read an account of how the hardships of war had at least in some respects been mitigated for nowadays the wounded were borne swiftly away in luxurious ambulances, even on Rolls-Royce chassis. This was not a Rolls-Royce. It was a very old Ford and the road we were travelling on, the road from Plugstreet Wood, had been frequently shelled and roughly repaired. We arrived at what I suppose would be described as a dressing-station, in the kitchen of a house on the outskirts of Armentieres.

I was carried in on a stretcher and put first on the floor where I was given an anti-tetanus injection. Then the stretcher was lifted onto the table. It seemed a very long way from me, from my head, to the foot at the other end of the stretcher or table. From the moment of the explosion to the moment I was put into the old Ford ambulance, I had felt absolutely nothing at all in my left leg and foot. The journey in the old ambulance on the rough road had woken it up a bit, but this was no serious pain.

This state of affairs was going to be brought to an abrupt end. The surgeon, a New Zealander, said, 'I'm sorry, I'll have to take that off.'

I said, 'Yes, I know that.' Then, as he advanced with what looked like a large pair of shears, I had a moment of panic and said, 'Aren't you going to give me anything?'

He said, 'No old man, I'm sorry. I can't.' His orderly got a grip on my leg. I got a good grip on the edge of the table on either side, and he cut. While he cut I had time to say 'My God' four times, half prayer, half protest.

Suddenly I had a nasty feeling that I had not been quite worthy of the badges I was wearing: Talavera, Gibraltar. I said, 'I'm sorry, I'm not very good at this kind of thing.'

He said, 'You aren't doing too badly.' Then they lifted me down, put me on the floor, and gave me a cup of what I think was Glaxo, or was it Horlicks? The South African NCO was now on the table. As I looked up from my rather odd angle on the floor, he looked simply ghastly and I thought, 'That poor devil is dying. Why oh why didn't they deal with him first? I could quite well have waited.' In fact he was not wounded at all; he was suffering from shock. The next morning he was eating a good breakfast and so was I.

Back into the ambulance we went and this time the surgeon came with us. On the way I said to him, 'Why didn't you give me anything? Is the stuff scarce? Are you saving it up for the big show that's coming?'

He said, 'No. You've had a severe shock. You're going to have a big operation. It was better not to give you anything in between.'

The Field Hospital, in huts, was somewhere near Steenwerke. They cut my clothes off and at 5.30 carried me into the theatre. It must have been about 12.30 when I was wounded. How had five whole hours passed? The only stage that had seemed long to me had been the time during which I was being carried, a time which must have seemed much longer to the carrier. Had I perhaps been longer at Armentieres than I had realised, asleep or unconscious? This puzzles me; I cannot solve the problem. Field Hospitals had no special room in which to administer the anaesthetic. I was carried in and put straight onto the table, with all sorts of grisly-looking instruments about.

As I was carried in, I thought, 'What does it matter if I don't come out again. I feel barely alive now. Why do they take all this trouble? I'm never going to be a whole man again.' There were no blood-transfusions in those days. There could not have been very much blood left in me.

At 9.30 I came round in the ward. For the first 48 hours after an amputation the pain is terrible, or was in those days. It's overwhelming. After that it begins to diminish, just a little bit, but quite definitely. But the beginning is terrible. The whole world is just one mighty pain. We all know how a nerve in a tooth can hurt. Every nerve in my leg had been severed. I had a toothache with the diameter of my leg.

When I was not sleeping or dozing I could still think. I began to have some small realisation of what Calvary had meant. We are so accustomed to seeing more or less standardised crucifixes that we do not really think about them. Some are made so pretty-pretty, that the makers of them must be thinking of Calvary only as a kind of symbol. But it was not a symbol. It was something horribly real, at least for the three men on their crosses. However, when a chaplain appeared and asked if he could do anything for me, I asked if he would celebrate Holy Communion for me. He did, and never has any Communion

Service meant so much to me as that one did. Often I have thought of that and of the contrast between my behaviour then and on another occasion, when a chaplain came to what was supposed to be my death-bed.

It had been in Gallipoli. Very very slowly I had tottered down the long communication trench that led to the beach at Anzac. At one point I overtook an Australian who had his arm round a man to take the weight off his feet. They were moving even more slowly than I was. As I overtook them and for a short time we were all in a line, the Australian turned his head, looked at me, and said, 'Like the other arm chum?' That was their spirit.

I was taken out to a hospital ship and soon was in a bunk between sheets. I was told I could go to the bathroom and have a bath. Only later, in Alexandria, did I realise that patients with typhoid or paratyphoid must lie still; they must not sit up or bend. Perhaps they thought a clean corpse would be pleasanter to handle than a stinking one. After the lights had been dimmed the matron herself came to see me. She spoke very kindly and all but kissed me 'Good Night'. Presently the chaplain appeared and asked if he could do anything for me. I said, 'No thank you.' The poor chap went away, no doubt to pray for me.

Why had I behaved so differently on that occasion? I think the shock of the horror of Hill 60 had been too severe, those horrible corpses melting in the sun, swelling, bursting, disintegrating. I had not lost my belief in the existence of God. Atheism had always seemed to me silly and still does. I had lost, at least for a time, my belief in the goodness of God.

Other memories were all too fresh, such as the death of Heywood, a fellow-subaltern in the same company. I was the last person to speak to him. I had warned him about danger ahead, then went on ahead to the head of the party. There was the sharp crack of shrapnel, a shout 'Sir, Sir, Mr Heywood's been hit.' I ran back. Heywood had taken a bullet straight through the heart. We buried him that night. Two or three of us were allowed to go down each by a different route, at a slightly different time, each with an escort. At the appointed time we all came forward out of the darkness. Hastily the Padre said the essential prayers. Heywood had no coffin. He was buried in a blanket. We stood round, each with his escort behind him. We faded away into the blackness. To me this had seemed beautiful, moving, the perfect soldier's funeral. I hoped I should be buried like this, in the night, no flag, no shots, no bugle. Darkness and armed men.

Heywood had been hit in the morning. We buried him that night. In between an odd thing had happened. I was bringing up to the battalion the party of a hundred men who had been working at A beach. Following the Norfolk and Suffolk brigade, whom we had found on the hills facing across the Gulf of Saros, we had marched all through Saturday night, spent a restful Sunday at Lalla Baba, then marched through Sunday night and now here we were to the north of Anzac.

To get to the battalion in the hills we had to follow a gully, which was dangerous only at one point at which one side was shallow and the Turks in the hills could see into it. I had been taken over the ground early in the morning and had come back to bring the party up. I had halted them before the danger spot, and it was then that Heywood was killed. Coming out from behind the safety of a rock face, they sprinted in small groups across the dangerous bit. After that they would be quite safe.

I went with the last group. At that moment another burst of shrapnel arrived, in fact several. I dived into the nearest hole. Unfortunately a sergeant chose the same hole which was not big enough for two. There we were, wedged, laughing absurdly; while the bush in front of us fairly rattled as bullets passed through it.

As we sorted ourselves out, the knees of a lad not far ahead gave way under him and he fell backwards. As we ran towards him, I saw a trickle of blood coming from his head and called to those already close to him, 'Take his helmet off.' They did and, as I arrived, brains fell out onto my boot.

As I looked down at him dead at my feet, I remembered it was Monday morning, wash-day. I had a clear vision of a Northamptonshire cottage and of a mother hanging out the washing. She didn't know that her son was dead but she soon would know. He was dead, here, at my feet, with his brains spilling out. I laughed. I laughed at the futility and stupidity and wickedness of the whole business. The Turk who had killed him did not know he had done it; he would never know. He certainly had not the least personal hatred for the fresh, good natured-looking lad who was lying at my feet. I laughed, with the laugh of a man sickened by the world's stupidity.

In the evening my company commander, Captain H.L. Wright, spoke to me. In peacetime he was a solicitor at Daventry and he was a very nice man. He said that complaint had been made to him that I had been brutally callous. I had laughed when a man had been killed. I explained. I was angry. I said, 'You've known me for nearly a year. I thought you knew me better than that.' All ended well, but oh! how pitifully easy it is to misjudge people, how misleading evidence can be!

As I lay in my bunk, in the ward of the ship, all manner of other memories came back to me. I was in high fever and my whole life seemed to race past at unbelievably high speed, happy memories of childhood in the country, happy memories of schooldays at Cheltenham and Bedford, happy memories of King's, my boyhood's love, my wonderful friendships, the kindness of older men, of my housemaster, form-masters, headmaster, of Brooke and Monty James, the Provost. In spite of the everlasting cares about money, life had been good. Now they had sent the chaplain to me; they expected me to die tonight. Tomorrow I should be dropped into the Aegean. This was utterly distasteful to me. I did not want to feed fishes in the Aegean. I felt a most intense and quite absurd longing to die in England, to see England once more, even if it were only for five minutes, before I died. This was absurd. Only the other day, when we buried Heywood, I had thought I would like a funeral like that. I was not wanting then to get back to England. Now I did. I think it must have been because I was on a ship, on a ship in movement, moving away from Anzac, from Gallipoli. I was lying in a bed, between clean sheets, moving away from the flies and the stench, and I wanted to go on moving. I wanted the ship to go on and on until it reached England, and then I would be ready to die. The ship was not going to England, and as I am writing this it is fair to assume that I did not die.

I had a terrible pain in my head. So bad was it that I prayed as I had never prayed before, prayed that I might, please, die quickly and get it over. While I prayed, someone else was praying. The younger of my two sisters was living at Richmond. She had a dream. She was with my father on one side of St Peter's Street, in Derby. They saw me on the other side of the street, looking ghastly. They saw there was something badly wrong, they wanted to get to me to help me. They couldn't. There was always traffic passing, something in the way. She woke up and she spent the night praying for me. She had the sense to note down the date and the gist of the dream, and long after she told me about it. The date fitted. Her prayers were better than mine: I did not die. Though I still felt I could pray, I did not feel I wanted a padre. Why do people want priests when they die? A Christian professes to believe that God loves him. Why then should he be afraid of Him? Why does he need an escort, a master of ceremonies? A child runs quite naturally to a father who loves him. There is no need of any formalities.

This time things were different. As they had taken me into the operating-theatre I had felt it really did not matter a damn. Now that I was back, in spite of this shocking pain, I had no thought of death but, strangely enough, as the Padre celebrated Holy Communion for me, I felt close to Calvary, to Him who had suffered there. This mighty pain had brought me to Him. That did not mean that my faith would never waver again. But there must be moments that lovers, that friends never forget. This was such a moment, a moment of happiness.

The morning brought a sequence of visits, which moved me beyond words. They all came early, before their normal day's work had begun. Quite early, I think it was soon after 6, the sister came to tell me that someone had brought my kit and they would like to speak to me, if I felt up to it. It was Langstaff and with him had come the Flight Sergeant. When they had gone, I heard a lot about Langstaff. In the next bed was the Battery Commander. Some of his people came to see him, and they told me what had happened, and they told me about Langstaff. It was a 9.45 shell which had struck us, an unusually large one for use on land.

On the very day on which we were going to blow away the trenches in front of Messines, the Germans had decided to destroy this battery, and the Germans had struck first. By a freakish chance their first ranging shot had landed on the Battery HQ, this little farm kitchen. The shell had landed just behind the tall subaltern, who was looking over the Battery Commander's shoulder. He had been dissipated. They had found a boot, which could be identified as his, with a foot inside it. The Battery Commander had only a flesh wound in his behind. Both Fidler's legs had been torn off, and he had died there in the farm. The South African was not wounded but only shocked. The telephonist and the clerk had been killed.

When Langstaff realised the farm had been struck he ran forward and slipped across behind the battery. Presently told to get out, he went back to his car behind the other farm, then, when he was sure that everyone else had cleared out, he slipped back again, regardless of falling shells.

When someone realised that there was still some movement in the farm and went to investigate, Langstaff was found, sobbing despairingly, heaving up wreckage, trying to find me. He was told definitely to get out or he would be removed forcibly. All this the gunners told me. When the Colonel came to see me, I told him all this. Many months later, in England, I learnt that the Colonel, having himself got the facts from the gunners, recommended Langstaff for the Military Medal, which was awarded to him. Meanwhile I had decided that, if ever I married, Langstaff must drive me to church.

The Colonel was very kind to me. I still have the letter he wrote to my father. Very early there had been another visitor, dear old Blot. He had been on leave and had returned at midnight. Instead of going to bed, he shut himself up with his gramophone and played it all night to make sure he did not go to sleep, then, as early as he dared to present himself, he drove to the hospital to ask if he might see me.

Last of all there was Higman. One winter night at 25 Section they were saying what a fine fellow Higman was, how lucky we were to have such a commander. His only fault was that he was too perfect a machine. There was never a mistake, a hesitation. Everything was always done promptly and correctly. He would be a little more lovable, someone had said, if he were a little more human. As it was, the total effect was fine but a bit Prussian. That is what someone had said.

The sister brought him to my bedside. He took my right hand in his two hands. Regardless of the good sister, of the orderlies, of the other patients in this purely military hospital, he stood there and he wept. The tears poured down his big, handsome, noble face. I had wanted to tell him where the key of the safe was. I couldn't. I couldn't speak. We had had some bad moments together in the air; it was all over now. For what seemed a long time he stood there, holding my hand. At last he turned and went. He had not uttered one word.

With the big battle coming on, if it was possible to move people without killing them they must be moved. I spent only two days in the Field Hospital. On the third morning I was in a hospital train. How kind and gentle nurses and orderlies were! It hurts me to read that there is a shortage of nurses nowadays. Surely there must be something wrong with the heart of a country which cannot produce enough nurses, which suffers from a shortage of gentleness.

In the evening we arrived at Wimereux. Ambulances took us up to what was normally a hotel. We were two to a room. A young VAD probably fresh from England, opened the door, but she did not let go of it. She gazed at us, said 'Oh! you poor men, I can't think how you stand it,' burst into tears and fled. Poor lass! Soon more seasoned people appeared, and a surgeon. I said, 'Don't bother about my leg for the moment. Can you please do something to my back?'

The blast of the shell had squashed me like a concertina. I had probably been flung against the side of the doorway as I turned over in the air; all manner of things had fallen on me as I lay on the ground: the muscles of my back had been crushed and bruised. The automatic movement of the muscles in breathing was painful in the extreme. He strapped me up tightly and this relieved the pain at once. Before I left, two days later, he ripped off the adhesive strapping — I felt as though I had been cut in half.

Here too they would be wanting the beds. Once again, after forty-eight hours we must move on. Ambulance to the dock, the restful movement of the ship, then stretcher-bearers again. Mine carried me along a platform at which a Red Cross train was already waiting, and dumped me at the end of a line of waiting stretchers. I was lying quite still, with my eyes closed. Perhaps they thought I was unconscious, but I was not. The fellow at my head said to the fellow at my foot, 'Seventy more of the bastards!' 'Hell!' I thought, 'What a welcome home!' On the other side everyone, French and English alike, had been kind and gentle. In the train there was the same quiet, efficient gentleness as on the other side.

We stopped at Woolwich and the train was all but emptied. Only about a dozen of us were being taken to Charing Cross. I felt a perhaps childish pride in being one of the specially badly smashed people who were being taken on. At Charing Cross I was the last to be taken out. The metal gadget which holds the two sides of the stretcher apart had broken, I was told, so I had four men to carry me instead of two. These were very different men from the Dover couple. They were St John's Ambulance Men, rather older, very gentle.

Ever since I have felt a special affection for them. When I meet one in the street I feel I ought to salute or somehow make obeisance. Very slowly and carefully they carried me along the Charing Cross platform. With these four men around me I said, 'This isn't a bad imitation of a funeral.' The old chap in front turned his head and said, 'Well Sir, if you feel like that, you'll be all right.' They put me into a splendidly gleaming Rolls-Royce ambulance, the gift of the Baltic Exchange.

In it already was another stretcher-case and our escort, a gentle-faced elderly lady who looked as if she came from Chelsea or Kensington. Slowly, noiselessly we began to move. The silence was quite uncanny. After all, we were in London, at Charing Cross. It was a beautiful night in the last week of May. The ambulance was open at the back. Something fell onto my chest. I put my hand to see what it was — it was a beautiful rose. I raised my head to look out.

We were passing through a narrow lane, just wide enough for the ambulance, through a great crowd of people who were standing motionless and silent. In those days all men wore hats. All the men in this crowd had removed their hats. This was a great city saying, 'Thank you.' Very possibly in these days some damned fool would say something about hysterical people glorifying war. This silent crowd of ordinary, sensible Londoners were saying, 'Thank you' in the best way they could think of. Can anyone think of a better?

Presently I found myself in the 3rd London General Hospital, at Wandsworth. It was in the buildings and in huts in the grounds of a school, the Royal Victoria Institution I think. My luck was in again. The surgical wards were full. I was put in an Australian and New Zealand ward. I had been with Australians in Gallipoli; I had observed for Australian and New Zealand batteries in Belgium; now I was with them again. Never for an instant did they make me feel that I was a stranger, an outsider. Was it on the first day or the second day? I cannot remember. Up to now I had managed to keep a grip on myself. I had a most outrageous headache — had I been concussed? Something snapped. I buried my head in my pillow and burst into tears. The headache disappeared. They shifted me into a hut on the lawn by myself.

My good sister Mabel came to see me. What she thought of me I have no idea. I felt fairly and squarely beaten. I felt there was no more good in me. What use was I going to be to anyone? People spoke of the wonderful things that artifical limb-makers can do in these days. I did not believe them. It was peaceful out on the lawn. Men behaved like beasts, but trees were still beautiful. The chestnuts were in blossom. Is there anything in the world more beautiful than chestnut trees in blossom? Presently I was shifted back into the ward.

One day it was found I had erisypelas. Had someone used a dirty instrument? I was whisked off to an isolation hospital at Tooting where I was to spend months in a room by myself and to have another operation. Of that long period nothing really can be said. Day followed day, week week and month month. One day the matron brought in a visitor. As she went out I heard her say, 'It's creeping upwards. If it reaches the base of his spine he'll die.' For days afterwards, when the stump was being dressed, I used to peep over the sheets to see how high the tide was.

One day the door opened and in came a most distinguished looking General, Sir Frank Lloyd, commander of the London District. He obviously had no small responsibility and his days must have been pretty well filled. I was not now in a military hospital nor was I in a ward; I was tucked away in a room by myself in an isolation hospital some distance from the centre of London. Yet this good man had become aware of my existence and had thought it worth while to find time to come and have a look at me.

In the early days a tube was inserted into the hole in my right leg; the other end hung from a little tank of Dakin's fluid which hung on the wall behind my bed. Thus there was a steady trickle of fluid through the wound. I gather all this is long since out of date. This wound healed very quickly, so evidently at least Dakin had not done any harm. With the stump it was another matter.

In course of time, a long time, the erisypelas disappeared but the stump did not heal. They tried a brilliant scarlet ointment, they tried a vivid green ointment. Was I becoming a kind of guinea-pig for research purposes? The fact remained that the stump would not heal. They amputated again. Then it healed fairly quickly. As I came round after the amputation, I felt a violent tickling on my left foot and stretched down to scratch, only to realise that there was no foot there.

I went back to the 3rd London General to the same Anzac ward, and now at least I could get out and about. I had been wounded in May; it was now December. The first thing I did was to think of Natusch, the New Zealander who had picked me up and carried me away on that horrible day, the day of Fidler's death. Towards the top end of Regent Street, on the west side, there used to be a good jeweller, by name Vickery.

To them I went and asked them to make a silver cigarette case with the RFC badge on one side in enamels, and on the other side, likewise in enamels, the badge of the Canterbury Regiment, New Zealand, a rather complicated badge with a kiwi in the middle. Below was engraved the date on which he had picked me up and I had spoilt his bags. When completed it was addressed to him at his regiment. Back came a delighted letter in which he said he had been slightly wounded and was now adjutant of the New Zealand depot at Hornchurch. This conveyed nothing to me. The south of England I knew hardly at all. A few days later he called to see me, but I was out. I thought, 'That is the end of that episode.'

However, in August of the following year, 1918, we were going to be brought together in a most extraordinary fashion.

10. Back to Duty

On the southside of Wimbledon Common there was a fine house belonging to some people by name Chubb. Mr Chubb had nothing to do with locks; he had, I think, something to do with insurance. He was a self-made man. He said it was not easy for a man to make £1000 starting from scratch, but when he had made his first £1000 the rest was easy. Unfortunately I have none of Mr Chubb's ability. They ran this house as a kind of private convalescent home for about a dozen officers. On paper they were still on the strength of the 3rd London Hospital and I had the good luck to be sent up there. I was taken up in the landaulette, that extinct type of car in which the front part stayed put, but the back part could be folded down. Every morning this car brought people down to the hospital for massage. On the morning of my arrival, having been shown my bedroom, I was left in a cosy smoke-room or library. There was a big open fire. Through a French window I looked across a lawn to fine trees. Here indeed was peace. There was a knock and in came the butler, bearing an egg nog on a silver salver. He offered me the nog. I said, 'No thank you!' He said, 'I'm sorry Sir, I have orders to stay here till you've drunk it.' I drank it. It was good.

When not going down to the hospital for treatment or being

taken to the theatre (that was the *Chu Chin Chow* period) or perhaps for a short drive across Richmond Park, we spent most of our time in the big hall where there was always a splendid fire. From the windows we looked over miles of country. In the dip below was the farm from which came our milk. The floor was of oak, highly polished, very dangerous for the unwary newcomer who had not learnt how to navigate rugs. On my first day, with my foot still on the bottom stair, I placed crutches on the mat at the foot of the stairs and prepared to swing forward normally. The mat shot off across the hall at very high speed, with myself describing the wildest contortions above and behind it. Mats at the foot of stairs are always a danger for those who wear artificial legs.

At Moreton-in-Marsh there is a pleasant hotel, the White Hart Royal, in which King Charles I once slept. Arriving a little late for dinner, some years after the first war, eager to make up for lost time, I stepped off the stairs onto a mat in the hall and shot across the hall through the open door into the dining room. By about the second table was a waitress who fortunately had just set before two guests their plates of soup. I was travelling fast and in urgent need of an anchorage.

There was no other possible anchorage in sight. I flung my arms round the waitress and held on. She was a sensible person, well balanced physically and mentally. Taken abruptly by surprise, she flung her arms round me and held on. We supported one another until, with giggles and explanations, all was restored to normal balance and respectability. Somewhere Milton describes clouds as buxom. Our old VIth form-master at Bedford, the famous Sanderson, explained that 'buxom' meant that if you applied your finger to a curved surface and pushed, the surface yielded, but if the finger was withdrawn, then the surface returned to its original curve. I need hardly say that I did not apply the Miltonian Test to the waitress. Possibly Erasmus was acquainted with the word buxom. He liked the girls of Cambridge; he said they were fair, soft and yielding.

One day there was a spare seat in the car taking people down to the hospital for treatment and I went down to see my Anzac acquaintances. The ward was one of a row of single-storied buildings. At one end was a wide French window and a verandah. I was told the car would be back there at 12.50. At 12.50 I was sitting on someone's bed, chatting, when I saw the car arrive. I went out and got in. A frenzied chauffeur rushed at me and more or less dragged me out. It was the Queen of Portugal's car. She worked at the hospital every morning. I just had time to assume a detached air before she arrived.

I was not the only English officer in the Anzac ward. There was a fighter pilot who had been wounded but had lost no limbs. He had, however, been in bed for some time. There was in the ward a very attractive VAD. One morning when she was dusting the locker beside his bed she said, 'In a month's time I'm going to be married.' He said, 'I think that's a great mistake.' 'Why?' she said. He said, 'I think it would be a much better idea if you married me.' She did. It should be said that nurses wore no jewellery in uniform and she was not wearing her engagement ring. He was biding his time, intending to propose when he was up and about. Taken completely by surprise, he reacted with the swiftness of a fighter pilot.

I moved on to Dover House which was the officers' section of the great Roehampton hospital. It lay behind, entirely secluded in what was then a country estate on the edge of London. We went down to the fitting-room by a quiet walk under great trees. If the garden did not provide scope enough for us, we could explore Putney Heath and Wimbledon Common. This spacious house has been swallowed up in a very fine LCC housing estate. Though it is a little sad to think that no-one will ever again look down that great green stretch towards London, the estate is certainly a notable example of good modern planning.

Roehampton House, the Hospital, was at or near the top of Roehampton Lane. On the other side of the lane, adjoining Richmond Park, was the Roehampton Club, in whose grounds were the wooden hutments of the Balloon Depot. To one side, adjoining the lane, lay the Club House, a pleasant building with a little formal garden in front of it. There had been changes at the Depot. MacNeece had been brought home from Belgium to take command. He brought with him Higman as 2nd in

Command. Somehow or other they discovered that I was nearby, getting a leg.

A lunch was arranged at the Club House. That was a joyous occasion, a hearty wagging of balloonatic chins. But all good things come to an end, and the time came when Higman had to go off to his afternoon duties and for a short space I was left alone with the Colonel.

I said, 'Well Sir, anyhow there was one thing you didn't know', and I told him how the Adjutant had caught me with gumboots in Bailleul, how Jones had reduced me to a state of terror before I was admitted to his — the Colonel's — room, to be told I was to take over No 32 Station.

How the Colonel laughed! He said, 'My dear Hodges, have you never realised that I stage-managed that? Jonah was put there on purpose to receive you and get you all worked up. The Adjutant told us all about the meeting in Bailleul. We laughed over it, then decided we'd give you ten minutes' hell, before you were told of your promotion.'

Something else too I was told which did not seem to me to have any funny side. Higman told me that at the time I was sounded, the IXth Corps had decided that it would be a good idea to have a balloon officer on the counter-battery staff, always available to give advice on things from the balloon point of view, and they had asked for me by name. At the moment at which I was wounded the scheme had been approved; after I was wounded, the scheme was dropped. No other name was put forward. It was nice indeed to know that people at Corps HQ had thought well enough of my work to ask for me by name. Higman said, 'Would you have accepted the offer?' I said, 'Yes.' He said, 'Oh, you would, would you? Blast you!'

Now I had hurt him, disappointed him. We had had hectic times together. If I was not exactly a hero for him, he had had complete trust in me. Clearly in his opinion my place was in the air, and from time to time he would have come up with me. I had been willing to break the partnership for what must have seemed to him an unworthy bribe.

But it was not really like that. I had begun to take a real professional interest in the whole business of soldiering. Just when I was applying for a regular commission it would have been a useful experience to work with the gunners at Corps HQ. It was too late now for explanations. That 'Blast you!' was an expression not of anger but of disappointment. I had hurt the feelings of one of the finest comrades I had ever had. That accursed 9.45-inch shell which had burst less than two paces from me was still doing its evil work.

So I felt then, nearly 54 years ago. Has it in the end all been evil? It forced me out of the army, though I have never lost my interest in the army; I have been happy as a schoolmaster. In the long run construction is more satisfying than destruction. To help is better than to hurt. But those who create and help would surely do well to think occasionally of those devoted men behind whose protection they can live their comfortable and useful lives.

In the hall of Dover House was an organ, which could be played by means of perforated rolls, like those used in pianolas. Among the patients was a sapper who had some understanding of music. We sat close together, pumping, he with his left foot, I with my right. The result was a considerable volume of sound. What real music-lovers would have thought of it, we never stopped to consider. It was a cheerful noise. In a world of unipeds, anything cheerful is welcome.

The tale was told of a patient who had a Ford. One day he took three fellow-patients for a drive. Somewhere near Guildford a lady collided with them, without doing serious damage. The driver, with one leg missing, got out. A passenger, with one leg missing, got out. A second passenger, with one leg missing, got out. The third passenger, with one leg missing, got out. The lady driver then had hysterics.

At meals we all sat at one long table. At one end was the Matron, at the other the Commandant, an old colonel. At his right hand sat the senior patient, also an elderly colonel. Both had done much service in India and loved to talk about it. As they did so, they forgot all about time.

Theatre managements were very kind in sending us tickets for matinees. If lunch finished punctually, we could just catch a bus at the end of our drive which took us to Putney Bridge Underground Station. We could not move until the Colonel did. If the two old dears settled down to talk about India, we had had it. We should miss our bus and our matinee, for on crutches one cannot really come crashing in late to a matinee. One evening, as we finished our performance on the organ, the sapper said: 'We must put an end to this India business. If they start tomorrow, every time they mention Poona I shall call out the score.' I besought him not to be such a fool and thought no more about it. The next day, when lunch was finished, the two old colonels started.

Suddenly a voice rang out clearly beside me: 'One!' Poona had been mentioned. In vain I nudged and protested, fearing an explosion. Nothing would stop him now. All the rest of us were silent. Presently came 'Two!' loud and clear. But the colonels were intent on their own affairs, lost in their own world. He got as far as 'Fourteen!' before they realised what was going on. We had no more trouble.

Now came long weeks at home, running in the leg, going down to Roehampton from time to time for adjustments, or to London for a Medical Board. Jock, the tawny old dog, was worried because I could not take him for his usual long walks. All day long he was with me. One hot day I was reading the paper in my father's study, sitting in grandfather's armchair. The doors were open. I was not wearing my leg. There seemed to be something odd about my foot; it felt oddly warm. But there was no doubt about it. My foot was oddly warm. I looked down.

Across my foot lay a freshly killed rabbit. Looking up at me, waiting patiently, stood dear old Jock, wagging his tail and looking a little self-conscious. Worried because I could not wander about the fields as I had done in the past, he had gone out and killed a rabbit and brought it to me. He wanted to comfort me. He was much too polite to disturb my reading. He had not pushed his nose into the newspaper. He had laid the rabbit across my foot, and then he stood and waited.

For a time I used a bedroom which my elder sister had occupied when she was at home. It faced eastwards over the fields to the rising sun. Below me was the kitchen-garden, then two large flat fields in which were always either cattle or sheep and, in the spring, the lambs. Buried in trees was a big Georgian farmhouse; further away, three-quarters of a mile away was the tower of Barrow Church, seen over the roofs. In the seventeenth century the tracery had been bashed out of the east window, in the eighteenth tombs had been used to mend roads; but it was still a beautiful parish church. Below the bedroom window a pear tree grew against the wall, trained upwards on both sides of the kitchen window, and brought together again below the window of my room.

We had a greatly loved tabby cat. She had been named, Heaven knows why, Jehoshaphat. As this was too much of a mouthful, she was always known as Josh. Josh used to go for walks with us up the fields, with her tail sticking straight up in the air. When she thought she had gone far enough, she just turned around and walked back. One night I woke suddenly and as I woke I felt sure I had heard a thud. I thought, 'Someone is in this room, and here am I in bed with no leg on.'

Outside the door of this room was the back staircase, then a thick baize door, which cut it off from the front landing and the rest of the house. My parents' room was up two more steps, through two archways, round a corner, in the south-east corner. Their windows faced south. They would not hear whatever happened here in my room. No other member of the family was at home. I was isolated. We had no electric light.

Very slowly and carefully I stretched out my hand and felt for the box of matches. Very carefully, taking care not to make the least sound, I opened the box and took out a match. Suddenly I sat up in bed and struck a match. The room was empty. I thought, 'Hell! the fellow's under the bed.' Carefully I took another match and leaning right out of bed, struck it. I was looking into a pair of eyes. Josh said, 'Miaou!' With her she had a freshly killed rabbit as big as herself. The dear old lady had brought it up the pear tree. The floor under the bed was covered with linoleum. I couldn't be bothered to do anything about it. In spite of most unpleasant rending and scrunching noises just under my head, I was soon asleep. In the morning I looked under the bed; the linoleum was spotlessly clean. Evidently Josh had removed the skin by the same route, down the tree.

Why had Josh done this? Did she think that Jock's way of expressing sympathy was a good one, worthy to be copied? Or was it just bravado? Did she want to show that a little old lady could do it just as well as a great hefty dog, in fact better. After all, Jock had not carried his rabbit up a pear tree!

Sometimes I went up the fields with a book. Through the second field ran a brook. Over it was a little brick bridge and on the far side a pleasant bank below a thick hedge. Here one could lie comfortably at peace. When I was on crutches, Jock walked carefully beside me. He never got in the way, he never tripped me. When we reached the bank, he took charge. He sat down beside me. No matter how long I stayed there, he never moved. During the summer, either in the garden or in the fields, I read the *Canterbury Tales* and all the plays of Shakespeare. School and Higher Certificate had ruined Shakespeare for me. I had never looked at him again. Now, in a nicely bound edition, with no notes at all, I found rest and enjoyment, escape for a time from the world's beastliness. Sometimes I just lay on the bank and watched the clouds drift by, and listened to the little sounds of insects in the grass, or the lovely, friendly, homely sound of a bumble-bee. No matter what part of the field the herd was in, sooner or later the cows would graze their way towards us, drawing closer and closer, till they formed a tight semi-circle. Then those at least who were in the orchestra-stalls lowered their heads, stretching their necks, to have a good look at us.

Jock sat quite still, with as saintly an expression as a dog can assume; he would even let a cow lick his nose. But if a cow, as cows do, suddenly sent forth a great blast of warm breath, that was too much for him. He jumped up barking, and shooed them away. They rarely, if ever, came back again. But they would be there again the next day and the day after that. It was a regular daily ritual, something to be done once. They made it plain that they did not resent our presence. On the contrary, they rather liked it. How did they decide on any given day that the time had come to pay their respects?

The periodical *Land and Water* published a similar journal of which I have forgotten the title, dealing not with aircraft but with those who handled them, with the human side of airwork. This was edited by Hilaire Belloc. There was always a page of verse. It struck me that there was never anything about balloons and I felt this gap ought to be filled. So I concocted the following and sent it in:

The Machine Gun

Balloonatics all hate one sound, which is to them detestable.
It mars for them the pleasures of an afternoon delectable,
And brings them moments of regret entirely unforgettable.
It is a brute.

When this is heard, their curses loud proclaim they are distinctly bored.
They seize their maps, then hastily on either side leap overboard.
They hurtle earthwards, praying hard, suspended from a hateful cord.
They parachute.

On cloudy days most frequently observers' minds it agitates.
Then safe approach and sudden dive the crafty Hun anticipates,
As, flying westward all unseen, his foul designs he meditates,
Balloons to shoot.

For this effusion I received a cheque for seven shillings and sixpence, signed by Hilaire Belloc. Stupidly, being hard up, I cashed it.

At last I could wear the leg every day, no more adjustments were needed. I had a spare leg too, and a medical board passed me as fit for duty. But they would not let me go overseas again. I had got to stay at home on the ground.

A tender picked me up at Chingford station and took me up to Loughton. This was a remarkable place. Epping Forest penetrates right into London. Almost all the way we drove through forest and ended up in a real village, with one or two largish houses about it. A tiny mess of about half-a-dozen was billetted in the spacious country house of a banker. The panelled rooms contained the barest essentials of furniture. My own room contained nothing but a camp-bed and a canvas bowl on a box. But the billiard table had been left in place. On fine evenings we could sit on the terrace overlooking neglected gardens. We could even play mild golf in the park.

This was a special depot for the training of balloon-crews for the balloons of balloon-aprons around London. The balloon-apron was a new invention. An apron consisted of three balloons in line linked horizontally by a cable from which hung vertically a number of fine steel cables, weighted at the end. The whole formed a kind of fence in the air. In conjunction with fighter squadrons these aprons were very effective. The fighters dealt with the gaps where the aprons were not, for instance, where the main roads or railways ran out of London. Where the aprons were, they forced raiders to keep high and there the fighters were waiting for them.

The crews which were going to handle these balloons round London did not need to be as highly trained as those who were going abroad. For part of the training I was glad to join them. There were fishermen on the strength. Alas! I have long since forgotten all they taught me, with one exception — a knot I use for the attachment of one part of the sling of my leg. Until the leather has actually worn through it never slips or gives way.

The RAF had come into existence and we were no longer part of the Army — the RFC was dead. Those who preferred to do so could remain seconded from their regiment. I did so. Ever since Gallipoli I had felt I was held to the Northamptons by a very special bond. They had made me a Captain and very soon after I had arrived in London in hospital in May I had been promoted Balloon Commander. This rank was never granted to anyone in this country — it had to be earned in the presence of the enemy.

Somehow the previous OC had allowed mess funds to accumulate, which seemingly just ought not to exist. They must be got rid of and this was to be done by a great jollification. He came along himself on the appointed evening, bringing some comely young ladies with him. There was abundance of champagne. Late in the evening, as a fair lady looked at me across a champagne glass out on the terrace and drank to *L'Amour*, I felt homesick for my peaceful Derbyshire home in which, as in many others, rationing made itself felt.

Here were people eating and drinking expensively simply in order to get rid of money and close an account. I had heard from my father of the kindness of one of his churchwardens who evidently must have thought father was looking a bit too frail. One day at lunch father thought he heard a scrunch of gravel. He went to the back door. There was no one to be seen, but on the threshold lay a large sack of potatoes. He hurried round the house and down to the gate and got there just in time to see the churchwarden disappearing at a gallop at a turn in the road. His horse had done well, but it just was not quite fast enough. I think it would be fitting to put on record the name of this good man — his name was Woodward.

Though life at Loughton and High Beech was agreeable, I was homesick, homesick for Derbyshire, homesick for Flanders and the old Wing. I had not enough to do. I had too much time to think, to make unpleasant comparisons between those who suffer and give and those who do not suffer and squander. I did not have to wait long. One morning I was put into a tender with my belongings and driven to a point somewhere east of Barking, to a Squadron HQ. There I was told that I was going to No 1 Balloon Apron, which was on the north bank of the Thames, near Barking Creek. The ground, now a housing estate, was then so marshy that it was not possible to have all three crews in one camp. One crew had a camp away on its own, nearer the river. 'There's already someone in command of the Apron. We're sending you down there as a supernumerary to take charge of that outlying camp. I ought to warn you that the camp is a bit on edge. They are so very isolated down there. That's the real reason why we're sending you there.' Well, well. Possibly this was a compliment: at least here was something interesting.

The commander of No 1 Apron was a delightful man, by name of Knox, bursar of an Oxford College — I think Oriel. After taking his degree he had gone into the Regular Army, stayed in it till he could retire as a Captain, and then gone back to Oxford. He had contributed to the Hibbert Journal. I asked why, with an academic and philosophical mind, he had gone into the army. He said he thought it was not good for a man to spend the whole of his life in a university. He should get out and about amongst people who were doing things actively. After lunch in a hideous little semi-detached house, I got into a sidecar to go along to my problem camp.

As I approached the gate with mixed feelings, the Flight Sergeant gave me a fine salute and said, 'Good God, Sir! It's you!' This was a wonderful bit of luck. It was Flack, who had been the rigging Corporal in 25 Section. He took me round and I looked at everything and saw everybody.

Then we retired behind a hut and I said to Flack: 'Flight, I've been told there chaps are a bit on edge. It must be very lonely down here.' He said, 'Yes Sir, it is.

'But I want to tell the men something about you I've never forgotten, though perhaps you have. You may remember, when we were in France for a fortnight, you used to sleep in a sort of back kitchen at the back of a cottage near the balloon-bed. The guard slept next door in what must have been an old dairy or something of the sort. Well, one night, there was a fellow with an awful cough. In the middle of the night the door opened and there you were. You gave me a tin of little black hellish-hot things, called "Meggoids", and you said "Corporal, give these to the chap with the cough. Tell him they're all I've got and ask him to give me back what's left when he's finished with them." We never forgot that Sir.'

I felt ashamed. Ashamed for us all. Surely there must be something badly wrong with the world, with our English world, if men could be so impressed by such a small act of kindness. Ashamed for myself. This man's cough was keeping me awake and the guard awake. They all needed sleep and so did I. Was it in fact really kindness at all?

I applied here what I had learnt with the Northamptons. I saw everyone every day and tried to learn all I could about them. Flack, in peacetime, was a foreman employed by Hamptons who used to be beside the National Gallery and were bombed in the Second War. He spoke with enthusiasm of decorating contracts on which he had worked. A native of Norfolk, he loved his native county and was glad to revisit it when he could.

One Sunday night Knox and I were alone for supper. He started a philosophical discussion. He said I really must not say that God was both good and almighty. We argued all the evening. At last I went to bed. When I was in bed, my commanding officer appeared and, standing over me, told me again I must not say that God was both good and almighty. One or the other — not both.

The following morning I was up betimes and away to my camp. Among papers needing attention was a letter from a Rabbi, supporting an application for leave for one of the men. I gathered that if the man were not granted leave to enable him to celebrate this particular feast with his family, his future in eternity would be much less comfortable than it might have been. I rang up the mess. Had Captain Knox come down yet? Yes, he had. He came to the telephone. I explained the problem, suggesting that I should not care to endanger this man's future or indeed present happiness.

Knox's voice said, 'As long as you persist in maintaining that God is both good and almighty, I can't entertain any application for leave for yourself or for any of your men.'

'Very well Sir,' I said, 'for purposes of administration only I'm prepared to admit that God cannot be both good and almighty.' So the chap got his leave.

In a unit consisting largely of Londoners there was a sprinkling of Jews. There were also some Scotsmen brought down to take care of the winches. As the apron was stationary, we had no need of a mobile winch. We had an old steam-winch. Everything about it was spotless. Every part that could be polished was polished. A man could have shaved in it. For these Scotsmen a piece of machinery was as something holy. One of the first things I saw, when I walked round, was a mobile gas-plant, standing out in the open and exposed to all weathers. Our gas supply had been centralised. The gas was delivered in steel cylinders, as in Belgium. This mobile plant had become redundant and would slowly deteriorate. It stood here, forlorn, forgotten. This would all add to the cost of the war. We or our children would have to pay for it. I drew Knox's attention to it. He passed the word on upwards. A day or two later it was removed. I began to understand why these men were on edge.

The camp itself was a lonely enough spot. The winch-men could not even enjoy what company there was in the camp. To be close to the winch, instantly available at all hours, by day or night, they lived in a little hut right out in the marshes. Their rations were carried out to them there. They were quite cosy, with a little iron stove and a supply of coke. Every day, no matter what the weather, I made my way out along the winding track across the marsh. I sat on a bunk and they talked to me about Scotland, their homes, their children. One day one of them produced a nice little horse-shoe. I realised at once where the metal, duralumin, had come from but took care not to betray any surprise. It had in fact been stolen.

Next door to our ground or area of marsh, was a dump of the wreckage of Zeppelins. On the one side, towards our lonely road, it was within the area covered by our guard. Though the apron itself was guarded and patrolled, it was not possible or necessary to cover the whole marsh. It would be easy at night for one of our men to force aside a bit of the fencing, slip in, and pinch a bit of airship frame from which to fashion souvenirs for himself or his family. The Scotsman had no workshop, no workbench. It must have taken him some time to fashion this horse-shoe. Had he beaten it out on the top of the stove, using the stove to heat the metal? I asked no questions.

He said, 'Sir, we've made this for you.'

I said, 'That's very kind of you, but don't you think it would be a much better idea if you sent it home to your wife?'

He said, 'No Sir, I'll make another for her. We'd like you to have this one.'

I walked away full of tumultuous thoughts. I still have that horse-shoe. The thought of these men's families, the sight of the neglected forgotten gas-plant gave me another idea. I suggested we might start a Unit Savings Association, for the purchase of Savings Certificates. Knox passed the idea on, official blessing came down from above, and we started. The idea caught on — I gather other units began to follow suit.

It was obvious that our camp might have been better planned. One hut in particular was badly sited. I suggested to Flack that we should move it; with our Londoners and Scotsmen we had plenty of men of different skills — they were bored stiff, they'd be only too glad to do something to make life more comfortable.

Flack: 'Oh Sir! You can't do that! We're not in Belgium now, we're in England. You'd have to submit plans, to get authority from the Board of Works, from God knows how many other people. There'd be hell let loose.'

Sadly I listened. In Belgium, if a hut or anything was not in the right place, we just moved it. Now, in England, we were in the bureaucratic world. I think now I was feeble, but Flack was a decent, law-abiding man. This peacetime foreman knew the rules. He would be shocked if we did something irregular. Vanity triumphed. Yes, it was vanity. I did not want to lose the respect of this good man. The hut stayed where it was.

11. Towards a New Life

After the daily excitement of life in the air in Belgium, this defence job was dull. It was the enemy that had the initiative. All that we could do was to inspect everything carefully every day, then wait. Someone, I think the Squadron-Commander, had had an excellent idea. It was found that one of the balloon hands was a golf professional from Abingdon. He was put on to construct a golf course. Clubs were got from Gamages and everyone could play. There was room for only four holes, so we had to play twice round and one hole more. The course lay below the main camp of the other two balloon crews, who in fact lived mainly in a fine red brick Elizabethan house, the property of the town of Barking.

It is now a museum. After the war I read an account of its reparation, and the impression was given that the always wicked troops had done considerable damage. If this is true, the damage must have been done at a later stage. On every day that I was orderly officer I inspected that old house from top to bottom, every corner of it, and certainly no damage had been done. In the part used for cooking some whitewashing had been done, for obvious reasons of hygiene. To some purists this might appear offensive. In fact no damage had been done.

Our golf course had two splendid hazards. One was a large

rectangular pond, along one long side of which was a close tall row of fine elms. The ball had to be lifted over the elms and clear the width of the pond. The second hazard was unique. It was a large dump of the sludge produced by the gas-making plant, caustic soda. If you were unlucky enough to land a ball on it, you were faced with a problem. If, to reach the ball, you stepped on the dump, you found you'd wrecked the sole of your boot or shoe. If, probably with someone holding on to you, you leant right over the dump to draw the ball towards you with an iron, when the ball arrived it had lost all its paint and possibly some of its rubber. If you left it there, you had lost ball and hole.

When people had had some weeks of practice it was decided to hold a tournament, people drawing for partners and opponents regardless of rank. This was great fun. Well do I remember watching the Squadron Commander playing against a miner from the North. The Squadron Commander was reputed to be a golfer of some experience. He had an impressive bag full of clubs. He teed up very carefully; after a certain amount of preparatory ritual he did a fine drive, straight and long. Then came the miner. He teed up nonchalantly with no apparent care at all, picked up what looked remarkably like a stick out of the hedge, gave a mighty swipe. The ball, driven quite straight, went much farther than the Squadron Commander's. We were really a happy family; I was enjoying life.

Our little semi-detached had a thin wall between us and the other semi. In the room on the other side was a piano, placed against the dividing wall. On it the daughter at times played fortissimo, one specially favourite old tune time after time. We had acquired an old gramophone with horn. When the favourite tune was played, the horn was directed against the wall and the gramophone started. This behaviour may not have been Christian or gentlemanly, but it was effective.

For an already middle-aged man Knox was remarkably active. Small boys had developed the bad habit of throwing stones at our tenders. One day when a tender came down to fetch me for lunch, it was arranged that on the return journey I should sit in front with the driver; Knox would be behind. A stone was thrown; Knox took a flying leap out of the back, did a remarkable sprint down the road and caught a boy. I cannot remember if he smacked his behind. He lifted him up by his coat-collar, told him all the ghastly things that would happen to him if he ever threw a stone again, shook him and let him go. No more stones were thrown. The police had not been bothered.

It was necessary to find some better way of disposing of the sludge from the gas-plant. I was deputed to go and see a firm who disposed of London garbage a little farther downstream, at the end of our road, which ran parallel to the North bank, not far from it. I had always hoped I might find an excuse to go exploring eastwards. Now I had one. At first our dull, flat road remained dull and flat. Then it climbed quite steeply up onto the summit of what was a mountain of London garbage, which was still arriving. It could come by water. Far below us, quite a long way below, was the Thames. As a child I had known it at Oxford; I knew it at Westminister; as a little boy I had jingled in a hansom-cab across Waterloo Bridge. I knew it at Blackfriars and at Putney. Now for the first time I looked out from a height over the splendid estuary. I have wondered sometimes if I have too much historical imagination. There are scenes that move me too vividly, such as those connected with the life of Jeanne d'Arc. Here had sailed Drake and Raleigh, and the Dutch too. Here was one of the greatest waterways of the earth, and I was looking at it from the top of a gigantic rubbish-heap. Yes, they could cope with our sludge. There would be no difficulty.

Every afternoon one officer, if he wished, might go up to town. I did not do so very often. I was quite happy out amongst our marshes. One day I was standing on Barking station waiting for a train. In those days they were steam up to Barking, then electric, part of the normal underground system. I was wearing the new RAF uniform, khaki with pale blue rings, and I was now a Captain. Not far away was a New Zealand Captain, complete with New Zealand hat. There was also a young pilot from some neighbouring fighter squadron.

The train came in, empty. The carriages were of the normal underground type, with sliding doors in the middle. I got in and walked down to the far end of the compartment. The New Zealander was talking continuously. The pilot was saying nothing. Apparently some tale was being told. I was not listening to their conversation. I happen to have, or at least I had, exceptionally fine hearing. All my life I have heard things I was not meant to hear. Sometimes this has been embarrassing, at others merely amusing.

Fortunately, as the New Zealander warmed to his story, he raised his voice. I heard him say, 'His bally foot waggling about all over the place.' Then he said, 'Absolutely ruined a perfectly good new pair of breeches.' I got up, walked along the carriage, planted myself in front of him and said, 'Excuse me, is your name by any chance Natusch?' He said, 'It is.' I said, 'I'm Hodges, the owner of the foot.' The face of the fighter pilot was worth seeing. He looked as if he thought he had got involved in some strange new confidence trick, that he was alone in a carriage with two knaves.

When Natusch had picked me up, he had been a lieutenant; so had I. Now we were both Captains. I was wearing the new RAF uniform. When he picked me up, he was not wearing a New Zealand hat. I had not recognised him. He had not recognised me. The pilot was quite unknown to both of us. Natusch had had his left-hand breast pocket lined with wash-leather, and kept his silver and enamel cigarette case in it. Waiting for his train he took out his case to light a cigarette. The pilot, standing near him, saw the case in his hand and the badges on it. He had the nerve to say to a complete stranger, 'I see the badge of my corps on your case. There must surely be some strange tale about that. Would you mind telling me what it is?' At that moment the train had come in. We went off together and celebrated. He wanted me to go down and dine with him in the New Zealand mess at Hornchurch. We were never allowed to absent ourselves in the evening.

That night or the following morning I told Knox my story; he passed it on upwards. It was thought so remarkable that I was given permission to go down to Hornchurch. In front of their mess they had a putting course and there we enjoyed ourselves. This was very different from Plugstreet! Presently he said, 'It's nearly time for dinner. We'd better go in.' As we approached the open door of the ante-room I saw it was full of senior officers and felt a bit scared. When we got to the door he stopped, and in an adjutantal voice said, 'Gentlemen!' They all stopped talking. Stepping aside and turning towards me, he said, 'Gentlemen, this is the man who said, "Cut the damned thing off. It looks very untidy." '

He maintained that those were the words I had used when he took my leg across his knee and I gave him my parachute knife. I had no recollection of this at all, but he stuck to his story. He said, 'A large number of officers have passed through this place. I lecture to them and I always tell them that story, as an example of the perfect military mind, which must have everything tidy.' We met more than once after that. In peacetime he was an architect. He availed himself of the right to be demobilised in this country and with another New Zealander won a prize for the design of a pub somewhere in London.

One night, when there was a raid, I was up somewhere near Chingford, I forget why. The raid over, I had to get back to Barking via Woodford and Ilford. It was pitch dark and raining heavily. Somewhere the driver stopped, uncertain of his way. The sidecar had an apron, but there was a hole in the middle of the apron. It acted as a funnel and channelled the streams of water straight into my lap. As the driver paused I said, 'My God, my feet are cold.' Never since have I known that strange sensation of feeling the foot that is not there.

At night we used to hear the clop-clop of heavy horses. I looked out. There were carts piled high with vegetables coming up from Essex farms. As a rule the man on top was fast asleep. How long had they come already and however long would it take them to get to Covent Garden? Hours later they would pass again on the return journey, the man on top asleep again. Where had they come from? How many hours had they been on the road? Surely these horses and men could not do their nightly journey to the heart of London and work on the land as well. They must be specialists. The men would be able to sleep, when an experienced horse knew the way and the routine, but not when a young, inexperienced horse was in the shafts. There would be no sleep then.

One day when I was out in the marshes I was called to the nearest telephone, which was at the balloon-winch. A voice asked if I had had any administrative experience. I replied that in 1915 I had been a member for a short time of a Brigade Quartering Committee and in 1916 had been Adjutant of a post in the Sinai desert. The voice said that on the following day I was to proceed to Felixstowe, where I should receive further orders. After a comfortable night in what had been the Felix Hotel, I travelled northwards in a Crossley tender through Lowestoft to Yarmouth. Here there were three squadrons, one of landplanes, one of seaplanes, one of flying boats. My luck was in. I was to be Adjutant of the Flying Boat Squadron. There were only two squadrons of flying boats in existence — one at Felixstowe, one at Yarmouth. These were former Royal Naval Air Service units. They still wore dark blue uniforms, kept on saying 'Aye, aye, Sir,' thought of themselves as Petty Officers and hated being called Sergeants or Corporals, and resented bitterly having been absorbed into the new RAF. Obviously a lot of tact would be called for. They had never had an adjutant before and had no idea what an adjutant was for. One day someone came into the Orderly Room and asked if he could have some nails.

At night all craft were put safely away in an enclosure which faced onto the sea and was guarded on all sides. But there was one exception. Between the sea, our enclosure and the Yare there is a spit of land on which stands a memorial to Nelson. Every night the pet machine of the commander of the Land Squadron was wheeled out there, when everything else was shut up. It spent the night out there, guarded and warmed up, so that if an emergency arose the Squadron Commander could run to his plane and take off.

Our Squadron Commander for the Flying Boats was Leckie, a Canadian, a first-rate man, a man for whom the British Empire was an inspiration, a man who could quote Rudyard Kipling quite naturally when talking round the fire in the evening. One evening in 1917 he and the Sea Plane Commander were still sitting talking by the fire, when an orderly rushed in with a signal for the Land Squadron Commander who had already gone to bed. Realising it must be something urgent, they snatched it from him and read it, before he took it upstairs. A Zeppelin was approaching the coast. They dashed out down to the Land Commander's plane, clambered in and took off. They shot down the Zepp and got VCs. When the Land Commander arrived, his plane had gone. It had in fact been taken by men whose job it was to fly seaplanes and flyingboats. Inevitably there was indignation as well as amusement. The two villains could claim that, as the Zeppelin was approaching, the one thing that was called for was prompt action. They were on the spot. They had acted. They got their VCs.

It is the fashion now to mock the Empire. Yet someone has said that the British Empire was the noblest of man's creations. Some churchmen would have us believe that the mediaeval church was a noble institution. It was never interested in freedom, in teaching men to think, to stand on their own feet. The Empire was. Wherever they went, our Colonial officers took with them justice, mercy, freedom, or at least education which prepared men for freedom. From time to time in my childhood missionaries visited our remote Derbyshire village and told us of their work in India and Africa. At Glyngarth, my preparatory school in Cheltenham, the headmaster — Bertram Auden — taught us to think of the Empire as a great family which it would be an honour to serve. He also managed to make us realise that children grow up, as the North American States had done and that, when the day came, we must hope that we should not be so stupid and obstinate as some of our leaders in the eighteenth century appear to have been.

In Gallipoli I had seen Indian troops and had worked beside Australians. In Sinai I had seen Indian troops and Australians again. In Flanders I had observed for Australian, New Zealand and Canadian batteries. Now I was ending the war with a Canadian commander. How lucky I had been in my commanding officers — MacNeece, Higman, Knox, Leckie and, before that, in the Northamptons, the great John Brown.

In 1945 when the second World War was over, I bought at the bookstall on Bedford station a copy of a Canadian illustrated weekly. This was the first and last time I ever bought a copy of a Canadian weekly. Some fortunate hunch or rather an old feeling of loyalty made me buy it. In it was a full-page portrait of the new Chief of Air Staff of Canada. It was Leckie. I wrote to congratulate him, and asked him if he still remembered me. He did, and he sent me a charming letter and a fine signed photograph. I am old now — what am I going to do with the visible reminders of old friends and comrades?

Leckie had such a strong Canadian accent that I sometimes found it hard to understand him. One morning, when he was going off for the day to some distant station, he poured forth instructions, then dashed off. I had no idea what he had said. Knowing the situation, I could only think out what orders I should give if I were in Leckie's place, and gave them. Fortunately our minds seemed to work in the same way.

There were half-hours of terrible anxiety. Of our three boats, each day one was being overhauled, the second was standing-by, the third was on patrol out over the North Sea as far as Borkum. If a boat, as sometimes happened, was overdue the tormenting question arose: 'Should I give the alarm? Should the second boat be sent out?' More than once, towards the end of an autumn afternoon, I stood alone, sick at heart, gazing out over the North Sea, listening intently. We never lost a boat.

I had a little trouble with my leg and had to go away for a few days to have adjustments made. When I came back I was still on crutches. A pilot, meeting me, said, 'Good God, old man, that was a quick job!' Meanwhile I had been posted away to another station but Leckie had said, 'No, Hodges stays here!' This was nice. Out of the blue came a letter from a man I had never heard of, Wynn, secretary of the Officers' Branch of the Ministry of Pensions, saying he had authority to invite me to join his staff as a personal assistant. I should be seconded from the RAF and continue to draw RAF pay. I replied I felt it was my duty to see the war out with the RAF. I had no intention of leaving Leckie and these fine fellows as long as they patrolled the North Sea.

Spanish 'flu descended on us. In many cases it developed into pneumonia, which in those days was likely to be fatal. Sixteen officers were taken off to the hospital at Thorpe, just outside Norwich, to a place which was normally a lunatic asylum. How unpleasant that description sounds, compared with the modern mental hospital. If my memory serves me right, only four came back. I was saved by devoted nursing and, apparently, by the fact that I normally drank very little alcohol. Leckie himself was abstemious. In fact everyone was, though wild and quite unjustified rumours were circulated about the drinking habits of the RFC and RAF.

When I came before the doctor who was to send me home on sick leave, I had a feeling that he had not looked through my file. He examined the top half of me and sent me home. The morning after my arrival I received a letter stating that at the end of my leave I should be A1, fit for general service in any part of the world. In reply I pointed out that my left leg had been amputated below the knee. Back came a rebuke. I should have informed the doctor that I had had an amputation. Why should I? He had not asked me any questions about my legs. He had had my medical history in front of him. Looking back now, in old age, I think perhaps I was a little bit naughty.

I had travelled from Yarmouth across country by a line which called itself, I think, the Great Northern and Great Eastern Joint Railway Company. It ran mostly through thinly populated country. In all sorts of little places flags were flying. I wondered why. At a country station I asked a porter what all the fuss was about.

The war was over, but not alas! our problems, nor the tumult in our hearts. At the age of twenty-five I should now have to face the world with one leg, and a knowledge of Hebrew and balloons.